TOM MITCHELL

1 MINUTE DOG TRAINING®

1 Minute Dog Training

Copyright © 2023 Mitchell Media, LLC. All Rights Reserved.

No part of this book or any images herein may be reproduced in any form without permission in writing from the author. Reviewers may quote brief passages in reviews. While all attempts have been made to verify the information provided in this publication, neither the author nor the publisher assumes any responsibility for errors, omissions, or contrary interpretations of the subject matter herein. The views expressed in this publication are those of the author alone and should not be taken as expert instruction or commands. The reader is responsible for his or her own actions, as well as his or her own interpretation of the material found within this publication. Adherence to all applicable laws and regulations, including international, federal, state and local governing professional licensing, business practices, advertising, and all other aspects of doing business in the US, Canada or any other jurisdiction is the sole responsibility of the reader and consumer. Neither the author nor the publisher assumes any responsibility or liability whatsoever on behalf of the consumer or reader of this material. Any perceived slight of any individual or organization is purely unintentional.

Cover design by keslehrman.com

ISBN-13: 978-1-7331645-2-8

First Mitchell Media LLC edition • August 2023

Dedication

To my two daughters, Malia and Kiana.
Your love of animals continues to inspire me.

To Samara; thank you for your love and support.

And to Linda Tellington-Jones, founder of the Tellington
TTouch, Robyn Hood, Mandy Pretty, and all the TTouch
practitioners worldwide for bringing awareness
and kindness to the world of animal training.

And last, to Michelle and Kea,
you live in my Heart and Soul.

DISCLAIMER
(PLEASE READ)

Tom Mitchell, 1 Minute Dog Training, One Minute Dog LLC, and Mitchell Media, LLC cannot be held responsible for any injury or damage resulting from dog training activities. If you are unsure about any aspect of dog training, please consult a professional in your area, or your veterinarian.

This E-book describes a proven training method for dog training. It does not cure dogs with aggression problems, or predatory aggression. Please ensure you take all reasonable precautions to prevent injury to others (including dogs).

While all attempts have been made to verify information provided in this publication, the Publisher assumes no responsibility for errors, omissions, or contrary interpretation of the subject matter herein.

Any perceived slights of specific persons, peoples, or organizations are unintentional. In practical advice books, like anything else in life, there are no guarantees! Readers are cautioned to reply on their own judgment, and those of outside professionals about their individual circumstances and their dog and act accordingly.

You will come across some suggestions and links throughout this book. As an Amazon Affiliate, this means I earn a small commission should you click on the link and purchase one of the products I recommend. You will not pay a higher price. Rest assured, I only recommend products that I use and love. They're all products my dog loves too!

TABLE OF CONTENTS

Foreword	1
Welcome	5
Welcome to a Breakthrough in Dog Training!	9
Chapter One Why Should You Trust Me?	11
Chapter Two What You Will Gain from 1 Minute Dog Training	16
Chapter Three Keep it Simple	22
Chapter Four What Stage Is Your Dog In?	40
Chapter Five Why I Created the 1 Minute Dog Training System	44
Chapter Six Why 1 Minute Dog Training Works	47
Chapter Seven Communicate with Your Dog Using the TTouch®	52
Chapter Eight Our Relationship with Dogs	61

Chapter Nine Leash Training with Compassion	69
Chapter Ten Why Do Dogs Pull on a Leash?	76
Chapter Eleven Why You Should Never Choke Your Dog	86
Chapter Twelve Chain, Prong and Shock Collars	88
Chapter Thirteen Is Your Dog Smart?	94
Chapter Fourteen The Dog's Brain	102
Chapter Fifteen Your Dog's Name	106
Chapter Sixteen Your Intention Roadmap	109
Chapter Seventeen Nipping and Biting	114
Chapter Eighteen The Importance of Play	120
Chapter Nineteen Woof!	123
Chapter Twenty Choosing the Right Dog Food	130
Chapter Twenty-One Choosing the Right Dog	136

Final Thoughts	**141**
Resources	**146**
Endnotes	**152**
Acknowledgements	**154**

FOREWORD

I've learned countless lesssons in my decades of experience working with dogs. In that time, I have constantly been reminded that each dog is extraordinary and a unique individual.

Like people, different dogs have diverse learning styles. One dog may respond well to something that another dog struggles to understand.

With the many scientific advancements made during my time as a dog trainer, we have learned so much more about man's best friend.

For all that we have learned, one of the biggest realizations is that we know so little about our dogs.

Like us, each dog has a one-of-a-kind personality. And with it comes a unique way of understanding the world. Every dog I work with teaches me and presents new surprises, challenges, and success stories.

There is no perfect way to train a dog. A simple, basic foundation of training and trust will help you build a relationship that can last a lifetime. That's what I hope to offer you with 1 Minute Dog Training.

All we can do is our best. We can listen to our dogs and strengthen our bond with them.

Be kind to yourself and your dog, even when it feels difficult.

It is an honor to join you on this lifelong journey!

Tom Mitchell

The 1 Minute Dog Trainer

I've been working with dogs since I was 2 years old. Helping animals has been a lifelong passion of mine. I'm so excited to share it with you!

SCAN ME
to Get Your Free Videos

VISIT
1MinuteDog.com

WELCOME

I'd like to thank you wholeheartedly for taking the time to explore this book. I realize there are hundreds of books on dog training you could be reading.

Given that you are taking a chance with this book, I want you to know how much I appreciate your trust in me.

My way of saying thank you is to give you a free video course. Please accept your free copy with my compliments. Visit **1minutedog.com** for free access to this exclusive program. Enjoy!

Watch How to Train a Younger Dog

Teaching a Child to Feed a Dog

House Training

Watch the Scared Puppy

Testimonials

When I first met Tom Mitchell in the early 1980s, I did not imagine he would become a lifelong friend, advisor, and someone responsible for helping to spread the Tellington method for companion animals across the globe.

For over 30 years, Tom has focused on helping people develop a relationship with dogs by promoting an attitude of kindness and gratitude for our canine friends. He clearly demonstrates that the the concept of having to be the the "alpha dog" has been thoroughly discredited by The American Behavioral veterinary Association.

Many studies have proven the effectiveness of the simple one and a quarter TTouch circles for reducing fear and pain and enhancing a state of well-being.

—Linda Tellington-Jones, Founder of the TTouch®
www.ttouch.com

I had a most positive training experience with the 1 Minute Dog Training! When I took my dog Buffalo to a local dog training class, they were too rigid and strict. Our work with Tom was perfect for both our temperaments....gentle and joyful, but firm. I highly recommend Tom, the 1 Minute Dog Training and TTouch work. There is a deep respect and care for animals and a positive life attitude that is a nourishing and instructive combination.

—Linda Reuther and Buffalo

WELCOME

Tom – Thank you so much! The 1 Minute Dog Training System really works! Our dog now comes with ease now because you taught us how to give him the right kind of positive reinforcement. I felt guilty not training him at least 15 minutes a day. Now it feels so much easier and more doable in 1 Minute segments.

—Char and Dr. William Showalter and Scooby

This is the best training method in the world! When my dog was young and I took him for a walk, he would pull me down the street. If he saw another dog, he pulled even harder. After a few short sessions, I was amazed that Mico listened and did not pull anymore. On top of that, he has matured into an awesome dog and this training played a great role in that. Thank you very much. I highly recommend the 1 Minute Dog Training!

—Basha Cohen and Mico

Check Out The 1 Minute Dog Children's Book!

As you explore this book, think about any children in your life.

The 1 Minute Dog Training system is a wonderful way to introduce children to the joys of dog training.

Roxy the super-dog also teaches responsibility and kindness along the way.

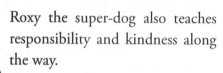

to Get the Kids Book

Visit **www.1minutedog.com** *for more information!*

WELCOME TO A BREAKTHROUGH IN DOG TRAINING!

"My goal in life is to be the kind of person my dog thinks I am."

- Unknown

This book can instantly help you create a deep and lasting bond with your dog. Here is a quick view of what we will learn together:

- How to develop a positive relationship with your dog.
- Effectively work with your dog in 1 minute sessions.
- The three simple steps to easily train any dog.

Almost no one receives a formal education on how to train a dog. You will discover the satisfying, step-by-step 1 Minute Dog training process.

You will be able to put your new skills into practice right away. It's easy enough that children love it—you got this!

CHAPTER ONE
WHY SHOULD YOU TRUST ME?

I was born on my grandparents' farm in Minnesota.

My father had built a tiny two-room house we called "The Shack." It sat above the tree-lined woods down the hill from my grandparents' house.

The Minnesota summers were spectacular, and the winters were severe. In the summer, I would pick berries with my grandfather and play in the mud. The winters were filled with sledding and playing in the snow.

It was a wonderful time and a great place to be a child.

My parents did not like dogs, but fortunately, my grandparents did. I was with my grandfather when I fell in love with a dog for the first time. Her name was Sandy.

Sandy and I were inseparable!

As an adventurous kid, I started to wander off as soon as I could walk. Many times, the only way anyone could find me was to call for Sandy.

She would come bounding out of the woods or a field, and usually, I'd follow close behind. I can still see her jumping through tall grass. We chased mice and snakes and ran together.

My love for animals—and my wanderlust—grew. When I was ten, we moved to Northern California. I spent the rest of my childhood roaming thousands of open acres near our home.

On sunny days, I'd take a snack and hike into the fields for hours. There, I discovered horses and ponies.

I'd follow them and slowly approach one with a piece of rope, trying to get it around its neck. Occasionally, I'd succeed and do my best to grab a mane and leap onboard.

To this day, I can still feel the sensation of riding through the fields until falling or getting bucked off.

WHY SHOULD YOU TRUST ME?

It was wild and risky, but my parents let me do it. It was magical. My love for animals continued to grow stronger.

Now, decades later, I've had the privilege to work with wolves, Olympic equestrian teams, zoo animals, aggressive house cats, and service animals, but my main love has always been puppies and dogs.

Throughout all the animals I have worked with, dogs have always been my special love and have shaped this unique method.

I have raised my family with dogs! Kea, our German Shepherd, was an important part of both my daughters' childhood.

WHY SHOULD YOU TRUST ME?

- 🐾 I have loved dogs for as long as I can remember. I've been training them professionally for over 30 years!

- 🐾 I have worked with many different animals all over the world.

- 🐾 My unique experience working with all kinds of animals has helped me to develop the techniques I will share with you.

CHAPTER TWO

WHAT YOU WILL GAIN FROM 1 MINUTE DOG TRAINING

The goal of this book is to teach you how to work with your dog in short, 1 minute sessions. This practice will show you how easy it can be to train a dog.

Without a simple guide to follow, many people think their dog is hard to train. They give up too soon.

Or worse, they think they need to choke their dog, hit them, or even…shock them with electronic collars to make them listen.

Dog training doesn't need to be complicated or time-consuming. You can become skilled at teaching your dog rather than hiring an expensive professional.

Most dogs want to learn. They just need our help.

Just 1 minute a day will make a difference. Two or three 1 minute sessions each day is even better. The best way to help your dog is by committing to work together regularly.

Why? Because in dog training, consistency matters. These 1 minute sessions will make that easy.

WHAT YOU WILL GAIN FROM 1 MINUTE DOG TRAINING

That's why the 1 minute sessions will work for you!

They are also fun for your dog.

These micro-sessions will hopefully become so rewarding that you find yourself doing several each day.

Within a week, you will have completed many 1 minute sessions and had a great time!

At the end of a month, you may have completed a hundred training sessions.

This routine especially works very well for children and families. So, recruit your loved ones to help too!

My daughter helped train our dog Roxy.

The more 1 minute sessions, the better. I have found that short, frequent routines will dramatically accelerate your results.

We will focus on training your puppy or dog with:

- 1 Minute Dog Training sessions
- Simple hand signals
- Gentle touch
- Kind communication
- Effective equipment

>CONTRARY TO WHAT MOST DOG TRAINERS TEACH…
>
>I RECOMMEND YOU SPEAK TO YOUR DOG IN COMPLETE SENTENCES RATHER THAN ONE-WORD COMMANDS.

As you train your dog, try speaking to him in full sentences. In my experience, people find it surprisingly effective.

This may be inconsistent with what you have heard from other trainers, but if you give it a try, you will find it works well.

When you turn blunt orders into complete, polite sentences—"Please come," "Sit down, please," "Wait, thank you"—your dog learns to pay attention in a different way.

I've found this helps them to become more grounded and more intelligent.

This way of communicating also demonstrates respect. And if we show our dogs respect, they will respect us in return. If you speak to your dog with harsh one-word commands, it may create adverse reactions.

Dogs have the capacity to understand us. They are so much smarter than they get credit for!

When we speak to our dogs in complete sentences, it has an impact. Dogs really can capture our meaning when we talk to them this way.

Stanley Coren, PhD is a famous dog psychologist who claims that the average dog can understand over 150 words. That's about as many words as a two-year-old knows![1]

Dogs are smart enough for us to speak to them in complete sentences—just like we would with a young child.

If you want your dog to be more intelligent, speak to him in full sentences. This is how he learns. It's how you learned. Like infants, dogs use their surroundings to understand the world.

Your dog will learn your tone of voice and respond to it. Let's say you tell your dog she is a good girl. If you yell it at her angrily, however, she will likely become upset.

Pay attention to the way you talk to your dog. Your tone of voice matters. Your intentions matter.

Before you know it, communicating with your dog this way will feel natural!

Every dog is truly unique. There is no "one size fits all" when training your pup.

However, with regular 1 minute sessions, you will develop an understanding of your dog's learning style.

In turn, your dog's skills will improve. The lessons you learn together will dramatically enrich your lives.

Let's Review

- Training your dog can be easy!

- Consistent, 1 minute training sessions will produce better results than longer ones, sporadic sessions.

- Speak to your dog in complete sentences! This shows respect.

- Your dog will also discover a new way of thinking if you speak to him in full sentences. This makes him smarter!

CHAPTER THREE
KEEP IT SIMPLE

What do your dog and your phone have in common?

They both have collar I.D.

1 Minute at a Time

I want you to have a great relationship with your dog - ASAP!

This system is inspired by research that has proven that reward-based training is the best way to train our dogs.

Like many people, I believe our dogs are valuable family members. I also know from experience that dogs are very intelligent.

KEEP IT SIMPLE

Training Fundamentals - The Big Three

The three things to teach your dog are:

- Sit
- Stay
- Come

In my experience, everything else will come easily once your dog has learned these three essential skills.

Your homework is to work with sit, stay, and come, 1 minute at a time. Look for little victories, and then build on them.

In those first training sessions, it's better to have fewer distractions. I suggest staying indoors before heading outside.

I will guide you through a detailed **sit**, **stay**, **come** training session in the pages to come.

First, I want to walk you through which training equipment I recommend. This is a short shopping list, and all of the products I recommend are generally low-cost.

It is very helpful to have basic training equipment. It's worth searching for these items second hand if you'd like to save some money.

With 1 Minute Dog Training, we primarily use:

A Flat Collar and Harness

A flat collar is what likely comes to mind when you think of a dog collar. With their basic design, these are great for displaying your pup's ID.

I use a collar where I have my family's name and my phone number embroidered. I recommend this approach instead of a dog tag because you know the ID cannot break off. If you got separated from your dog, someone could quickly contact you.

In some countries and some states in the US, you may still need to register and get a tag for your dog. Check your local municipality about this. Many people also microchip their animals.

While there are some concerns about microchips, it is the most secure way to make sure your dog returns home if she gets lost. Many locations require microchipping if you want your dog to be licensed, which may also be required.

According to the AKC, "Pets with microchips are up to twenty times more likely to be reunited with their owners if lost."[2]

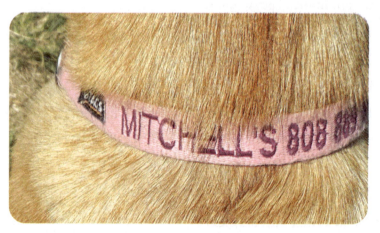

We have our last name and phone number embroidered on Roxy's collar.

Many people keep their dog's flat collar on at all times. You only want to attach a leash to your dog's flat collar for short trips, such as a potty break in your yard. For lengthier leash outings, I opt for a harness instead.

Does your dog pull on the leash? Many dogs do, especially in the early stages of leash training.

The strain this causes on a dog's neck can cause serious injuries. For walking your dog, a harness is much safer than a traditional flat collar.

Any time we take Roxy out, she wears her harness.

A harness has more material than a flat collar, fitting your dog more like a shirt than a necklace. They relieve tension in your dog's neck when walking on a leash.

There are many harnesses on the market. You can visit my website, **1minutedog.com**, to see the harness I use. I have found it to be durable and easy to put on and take off.

A Leash

You will also need a leash or long line to attach to your dog's collar, harness, or head halter.

For the DIY readers, you could easily use a piece of rope that is at least 10 feet long.

There is a lot of debate around the use of retractable leashes. There have been numerous reports of dogs and people getting injured from these kind of leashes.

A hyper or overactive dog can become hard to manage or control. They may even break away and harm humans if someone grabs the cord in an attempt to reel their dog in.

Even if you click on the switch to pull your dog back in, she may have enough freedom to do some damage to another animal, herself, or even run out into the road.

This is especially true if you are around wild animals (such as squirrels), other dogs, or particularly if your dog is not very friendly to people. My feeling is that you should not use retractable leashes while training your dog.

Treats

Most dogs are very motivated by food. Leverage your dog's training sessions with his love for snacking.

Once you and your dog get the hang of things and have developed a deeper bond, you can replace treats with free (and less fattening) rewards like love and affection.

In the early stages of training, I use small, single ingredient treats made from wholesome nutrients. I prefer to use organic beef treats. I usually break them into small pieces.

It can be challenging to find high-quality and affordable dog treats. You might be surprised to find a handful of dog-friendly treats inside your fridge. But, just be careful not to overfeed your dog.

One of my favorite ways to reward dogs with food is by rationing their dinner. Individual pieces of kibble are great treat alternatives if you feed your pup commercial dog food.

You won't pay a penny more than what you're already spending. Better yet, this encourages your dog to connect with you around her meals.

I think it's crucial to slowly wean off the treats when training and replace them with greater rewards: Touch, affection, and love.

You want your dog to listen because she wants to. Many dogs will only listen when you have treats. This is especially true for dogs who have been trained to come and rewarded continuously with treats.

You can shape this behavior by switching up which rewards you use. In my experience, your dog will prefer touch over treats before you know it!

We want our dogs to listen and come to us because that's what they want to do. That is the kind of relationship we want to have with our dogs.

Exercise caution when you share snacks with your dog, though. Many human foods can poison your pup. The most crucial ones (among others) to remember are:

1. Chocolate
2. Grapes and raisins
3. Onions and garlic
4. Xylitol (a sugar-free sweetener found in a variety of products like gum, candy, toothpaste, and sometimes peanut butter)
5. Macadamia nuts
6. Salt
7. Caffeine and Alcohol
8. Tobacco products and Marijuana

Sit, Stay, Come–Step-by-Step

The first skill your dog should learn is how to sit. Once she can sit when you ask, she is ready to learn to stay. Once she can stay in her seated or down position, start working on having your dog come when called.

After your dog knows how to come when you ask, you can practice **sit**, **stay**, and **come** all together in one short session.

To begin, have your dog sit down next to you. Please be patient if your dog does not want to sit or keeps standing up.

How to teach your dog to sit:

1. Gently touch your dog's chest to offer support.
2. Meanwhile, push softly on the back of her knees.
3. Add your verbal cue, such as "Sit please" or "Sit down (name)."
4. Once your dog sits, enthusiastically praise her!

Apply gentle pressure to the backs of the legs to protect your dog's joints. When a dog's rump is forcefully pushed into a seated position, it can injure them.

As you can see, I support Roxy's body as I help her into sit.

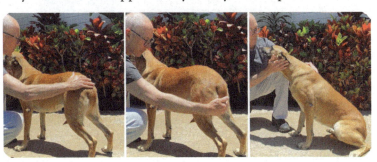

Very little pressure is needed, as this cue gently encourages your dog to sit.

Here I help Sunny the service dog, into a sitting position.

Another great way to teach your dog to sit independently is by "capturing" the behavior when it naturally happens.

"Capturing" is simple; it's the act of rewarding your dog for something he already does.

For example, let's say you are feeding your dog and he sits down on her own while you prepare the food. You might say, "Wow, way to sit, Buddy!" and praise him profusely.

This will train your dog to sit or lie down often to get praise. It also encourages your dog to strengthen his decision-making skills.

"Sit" should feel safe for your dog. Teach this behavior in a calm environment, and remember to keep training positive.

How to teach your dog to stay:

1. Ask your dog to please sit. When she does, reward her for doing it well. In the beginning, this can be done with a small treat. After a while, it should be done with praise and touch.
2. Walk about 5 feet away. If your dog keeps standing up, have a family member or friend help you. They can help your dog or puppy stay in a seated position.
3. Use your verbal cue, such as "Stay girl" or "Wait please," and a *wait* hand signal.
4. Take one or two moments to smile at your dog. If she's a puppy, she might wiggle a lot and want to come to you.

In many cases, I find it easier for dogs to stay in one spot if they are lying down rather than just sitting. This is not true for all dogs, and you will have to experiment with your own dog to see what works best.

To maintain your dog's trust in you, ask her to wait for short periods of time only. We want our dogs to *want* to stay when we ask them!

Showing your dog that "stay" is temporary will make her more willing to listen. And listening when you say "stay" could be a matter of life and death.

While your dog is in "stay," here is how to proceed:

1. Stay where you are, with about 5 feet in between you and your dog. Call your dog by name; let's say it is Bella. Say, "Bella, please come," and have your helper let Bella go.
2. When Bella comes to you, ask her to sit down right in front of you.
3. Praise and reward her for being such a good girl. In the beginning, give her a treat!

Of course, many puppies and most untrained dogs want to jump up on you. In training or re-training a dog to stop jumping on you, the first thing you want to do is to be aware of why your dog might be doing this. Puppies learn to jump up to lick their mother's face.

Dogs also become very excited if you've been away for more than several minutes. They want to make a connection. If you are working with this issue, it may take a few sessions before your dog learns. Please remain kind.

Jumping up usually means the dog wants to get as close to you as possible. It allows them to get closer to you.

Unfortunately for many of us, a dog jumping up is no fun! In my experience, jumping up will bring many problems, so you want to stop this behavior.

KEEP IT SIMPLE

The best way to teach this is to immediately and politely ask your dog to sit every time he comes up to you. If your dog does not go into a sitting position, help him to sit.

IMPORTANT

I also believe that your dog should sit down and wait before going outside, through a doorway, or out of the car.

It is best for your dog to get in the habit of waiting before you give them permission. This keeps your dog safe and your relationship strong.

I often change having a dog sit or lay down when they come. I think it's important that you alternate the two.

THE MOST ESSENTIAL ELEMENT OF DOG TRAINING IS THAT YOUR DOG COMES WHEN CALLED.

This brings up the question:

Why do dogs come when we ask them to?

The answer is…

Where you are is where they want to be!

So, you should never call your dog to punish him. If you do, he might become hesitant to approach you. This is the exact opposite of what you want.

I have worked with hundreds of dogs who don't come when called because they have learned that coming when called may cause pain or present a problem.

Your dog should come every time you ask. Why? Because where you are is where your dog wants to be!

Below, I've outlined what a **sit**, **stay**, **come** session looks like from start to finish. Repeating this daily, even just one or two minutes at a time, can work wonders!

These three skills are the key to your training success. Remember, consistency is the fastest way to get incredible results.

Sit, Stay, and Come
Practice Indoors First and then Move Outdoors

Step 1: Ask your dog to sit. You may need to show him by gently helping him into a sitting position (please refer back a few pages to the section *How to teach your dog to sit:*).

Step 2: Use a soft voice and hand signal and ask your dog to stay. It also works well to have your dog lie down instead of sitting if he has trouble staying put. Try both and see which is best. Enlist some help from a friend if you need it.

Step 3: Walk 5 feet away. Then, in an enthusiastic voice, ask your dog to come.

Step 4: When he does come, praise him and ask him to sit down in front of you.

If your dog does not come, have someone help you. Have one person sit with your dog as he sits and waits. You will back 5 feet away and then call your dog. If your dog is confused and doesn't know what to do, the person who is sitting with your dog can encourage him to go to you using their voice and gestures.

When you are doing this for the first time indoors or you do not have someone to help you, use a 15-foot leash or rope so you can give your dog a gentle signal on the lead to help him understand what the phrase "please come" means.

Continue to work with sit, stay, and come inside your house. The next phase would be to ask your dog to sit and stay while you walk out of sight and into another room. Then, count to five and call your dog. After that, your dog is ready to go outside and into different environments.

This is a great activity for kids if they are interested in helping train the family pup!

This is my daughter and our dog practicing Sit, Stay, and Come.

When you move outside, please make sure to use a long leash or be in a fenced yard to make sure your dog doesn't try to run off while you're training together.

I encourage you to practice sit, stay, and come for a few minutes each day.

Your dog will begin to understand what you are asking him to do and eventually once you feel confident your dog can sit, stay, and come, you can take off the leash and practice.

KEEP IT SIMPLE

Check out your free video package at www.1minutedog.com to watch training sessions in action. This visual guide can help you teach your dog. The video "Watch How To Train A Younger Dog" goes through the Sit, Stay, and Come Training Tips.

Watch How to Train a Younger Dog

Teaching a Child to Feed a Dog

House Training

Watch the Scared Puppy

Action Items

- Gather the training equipment.

- Work on sit, stay, and come with your dog.

- It's ok if he doesn't get it right away. You can further shape the skills in each 1 minute training session.

- Intersperse using treats and praise as you work on your dog's skills.

KEEP IT SIMPLE

- **Sit**, **stay**, and **come** are the first skills to teach your dog.

- You may use training treats early on. Then replace them with praise and physical touch as you practice.

- Your dog should come every single time you call. This is because your dog can't imagine anywhere better to be!

- Ask your dog to sit down as soon as they come when called. This prevents the bad habit of jumping up on people.

CHAPTER FOUR
WHAT STAGE IS YOUR DOG IN?

*"Dogs are not our whole life,
but they make our lives whole."*

- Roger Caras

Understanding where your dog is in her training journey prepares you for the road ahead.

On the one hand, an older or rescue dog may require calm sessions and more patience.

On the other hand, Puppies want to chew and will be distracted by everything for the first year or two of their life. Working with puppies requires shorter and more focused training sessions.

If you lose focus, as I have in the past, your teething pup might chew a hole in the seat of your brand-new car.

WHAT STAGE IS YOUR DOG IN?

Yes, that happened to me. It was a great lesson. She was not my dog, but I agreed to watch her for a few hours while my friend, Michelle, went to an appointment.

She was a beautiful six-month-old German Shepherd named Kea. She was smart, sweet, and still growing.

I picked up Kea at Michelle's house. Then, I drove back to my house to grab a few things before going to the park. I rolled down the windows of my new Acura. I really liked that car!

I told Kea I'd be back in two minutes and ran into the house. That was all it took.

She ate a hole the size of a watermelon in the leather of the backseat.

When I came out, she had her head hanging out the window with a huge smile on her face. She did not even look remorseful.

Of course, she was teething, as all puppies do at that age, and she was just looking for something to chew on. Should I have been mad at her? What should I have done?

When I was a child, I learned that people whacked a dog with a rolled-up newspaper if they made a mistake. Even when I was young, that never made sense to me.

Did you ever hear that was the way to train a dog? Well. First, never do that!

Second, I like the rolled-up newspaper concept in only one way: Instead of hitting your dog, you might use it on yourself with a gentle bop and say, "I will pay attention to my dog."

That is why I discovered a hole in the backseat of my car. I should have thought it through before leaving her alone.

- Pay attention to your dog! Any mistakes fall on you, the leader.

- Lead your dog with kindness, patience, and empathy.

- Puppies require different approaches to training compared to older dogs.

- Try to understand your dog's history and which stage of life they are in.

CHAPTER FIVE
WHY I CREATED THE 1 MINUTE DOG TRAINING SYSTEM

The more time I spent with dogs, the more I saw where we fell short in training them.

Like me and many others, you probably adore dogs. And chances are, you are eager to make the most of your relationship with your dog, but you may have come across some challenges.

Dogs can be some of our greatest friends and teachers. They live simply, love generously, and care deeply.

If we followed their lead, we would run to greet our loved ones the moment they came home. We'd never pass up an opportunity for a joyride, delight in the simple pleasure of a long walk, and never pretend to be something we're not.

The lessons dogs can teach us are endless. But frustrations—if not outright problems—often arise when we don't know how to teach them.

We snap at the puppy who's chewing on our shoe. We shout at the teenage dog who pulls on his leash. We grow impatient when our older dog takes too long to "do her business" and scold our pup when he begs.

We want our companions to be well-mannered, but sometimes life's demands keep us from training our dogs with patience and kindness.

The book you are holding is the solution to this dilemma.

In the past, I did one-on-one in-home training sessions with families and their dogs. We worked together on their dog training goals, and after each session, I gave them follow-up homework in the form of longer, 20-minute sessions they could do over a week.

We would always start with the basics of:

- Sit
- Stay
- Come

People would easily understand that concept. But when I'd return, they'd say, "Tom, we wanted to work with our dog, but we ran out of time."

After hearing this repeatedly, I started asking if they had just ten and then five minutes to concentrate on their efforts to train their dog. They would hesitate before saying, "Yes, we have five minutes."

And yet, even that seemed daunting for some people. I finally asked if they had 1 minute to work with their dog. Everyone enthusiastically nodded and said, "Yes, I can spare a minute!"

With this in mind, I created the 1 Minute Dog Training sessions. Amazingly, these proved more effective than the longer sessions I had used.

- There is so much to learn from dogs.

- We often struggle as their teachers. This is very understandable, as we do not speak dog.

- You are probably very busy. I am too, which is why this method was made for even the busiest families!

- Focus on the basics:
  - Sit
  - Stay
  - Come

CHAPTER SIX
WHY 1 MINUTE DOG TRAINING WORKS

How long did you go to school? Most of us go to school for at least twelve years. That is over 10,000 hours of school.

Many go on to college—roughly another 5,000 hours of education (not to mention those who pursue graduate degrees).

Isn't it funny that we enroll our dogs in a six-week training course and expect them to have perfect manners for the rest of their lives?

And then, we stop the daily training sessions and think our dogs will never forget what they learned in those six weeks. Those are pretty high expectations!

The truth is that many dogs genuinely want to learn. It's our job to help them.

Training your dog 1 minute at a time provides consistency. And consistency is the key to long-term success.

Some days, you might train your dog two, three, or even five times. On other days only once.

The most important thing is to stop for 60 seconds and work with these simple training techniques: sit, stay, and come.

If there are other people in your home, have them help you! Enroll them in the 1 minute sessions.

If you stick with these micro sessions, they will become a habit for you and your dog. This routine will strengthen your relationship and produce lasting results. Collectively, over time, you will have a well-trained dog.

I believe most dogs are inherently smart. If we give them choices and help them understand what we are asking, they will learn. Amazingly, it does not take them 10,000 hours.

Do you want your dog to learn even faster? Well, I have a solution for you. I have used a revolutionary technique in my training sessions for many years. It was developed by a woman named Linda Tellington-Jones.

WHY 1 MINUTE DOG TRAINING WORKS

My dear friend, Linda Tellington-Jones.

I've had the privilege of knowing Linda for over thirty-five years. I started working with Linda in the 1980s with horses.

This powerful method of communication, called the Tellington TTouch®, will enhance your daily training routine, and your dog will learn faster. You can learn about this technique on Linda's website, **ttouch.com**.

Action Items

- Work with your dog at least once each day - the more the merrier!

- Keep training sessions short. Spending just 1 minute working together can produce incredible results.

- Make dog training fun! A high-energy 1 minute session can be a blast for both you and your dog.

- If you do three 1 minute sessions each day, at the end of a month, you will have done almost 100 sessions.

- It's the consistency that will help your dog learn and help you strengthen your bond.

- Many of us go to school for 12-16 years or more. That is over 10,000 hours of learning!

- It's common for puppies to attend only six weeks of puppy classes. We expect them to be perfectly well-trained for the rest of their lives.

- If you train your dog for 1 minute each day, the results will be much better. Why? **Because consistency is key!**

CHAPTER SEVEN

COMMUNICATE WITH YOUR DOG USING THE TTOUCH®

I am pretty confident you would agree that dogs speak the language of scents, sights, noises, and instincts that have evolved over thousands of years.

Given we rely on different skill sets, how can we find a common language to deepen our relationship? There are several things we can use:

- Intentional touch
- The way we speak
- Visual cues
- A clear mental image of what you want to accomplish

In the following chapters, you will learn how to communicate with speech, physical, and visual cues to help your dog understand.

First, you will discover how to use special touches that help your dog learn.

So, let's dive in!

COMMUNICATE WITH YOUR DOG USING THE TTOUCH® 53

The Tellington TTouch® Method enhances the emotional, mental and physical wellbeing of various animals.

> "The TTouch has opened whole new vistas of opportunity for veterinarians. With it, we can reassure the stressed dog or other animal and help it to become a full participant in its own recovery.
>
> "Perhaps more important, owners can quickly learn to use the TTouch to form the same close therapeutic connection with their pets."
>
> —Tom Beckett, Doctor of Veterinary Medicine

It was initially designed for working with horses. I had the privilege to work with Linda Tellington-Jones in the 1980s in Europe with members of different Olympic Equestrian teams. We also taught other clinics together for dogs, horses, and zoo animals.

The results were so impressive that the Tellington TTouch Method was adapted to work with dogs, cats, humans, zoo animals, rabbits, small beings like guinea pigs, and birds. I know I am talking about horses again, but the commonality between horses, dogs, cats, and zoo animals is that they all respond to this type of touch.

Here is a testimonial for the TTouch from Art Goodrich. He was a master zookeeper from 1973 - 2000 at the world-famous San Diego Zoo. Linda and I had the privilege to work with him on numerous occasions.

> "I've never seen anything like the way animals respond to this method of handling. The TTouch reduces stress and pain, alters negative behavior, and speeds up the healing of injuries that haven't responded to other treatments.
>
> "I have used TTouch on everything from aardvarks to zebras. Giraffes especially enjoy the relaxing of the muscles and the relief of painful areas." He says that all the animals he handled received a measure of TTouch, and, "They all loved it and wanted more."

—Art Goodrich, Master Zookeeper at the San Diego Zoo

The TTouch work has also been featured on television including Unsolved Mysteries and many other primetime TV spots.

It may seem confusing at first if you've never heard of anything like this. Still, these intentional touches might completely transform your relationship with your dog.

COMMUNICATE WITH YOUR DOG USING THE TTOUCH®

There are tens of thousands of people worldwide who use the TTouch with great success: animal lovers, trainers, breeders, veterinarians, zoo personnel, and shelter workers to name a few.

There are also almost two thousand TTouch practitioners around the world, many of whom are excellent dog trainers.

To do the Basic TTouch Circle you gently move the skin in 1 ¼ circles. The mindful, circular movements of the TTouch are very therapeutic for your dog in many ways.

What do I mean by mindful? When you move the skin gently in a 1¼ circle, focus on the roundness and smoothness of the circle.

Taking approximately 2-3 seconds to complete each 1¼ circle will calm your dog and enhance her ability to learn and listen to you.

Here are a few fundamental, easy-to-learn techniques to get you started.

Pressure and Direction

Anybody can practice TTouch on their dog! It's okay if you don't know anatomy or massage techniques. You can easily learn how to improve your dog's well-being with these simple TTouches.

Begin by imagining the face of a clock on your dog's body. Place the imagined clock with the six o'clock toward the ground.

The size of your imaginary clock depends on the looseness or tightness of the skin. The circle on a joint could be as small as a quarter of an inch and on loose skin as big as one inch or more.

Start with your fingers at 9 o'clock on the imaginary clock. Move the skin in a clockwise direction, do a full circle back around 9 o'clock, and then go another quarter of a circle. Your fingers should end at 12 o'clock.

If you or your dog find it more comfortable with a counterclockwise circle, trust your feeling.

It helps to use your other hand to support your dog's body. This will help her to relax while doing the TTouches.

Experiment with light connection with the skin until you find what works for your dog. Your dog's body language will indicate how comfortable she is with your contact.

Circular TTouch

The most basic TTouch is done with the pads of your lightly curved fingers, as shown in the image on the next page:

You can also straighten your fingers a bit to make more contact with your dog's body. Do these TTouches with very gentle pressure. Refer to the image below:

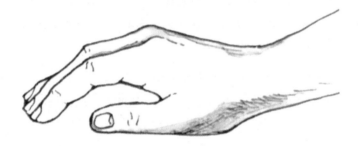

Your goal is to help your dog become a cooperative, focused, confident and trusting member of your family. In fact, the second T in TTouch stands for trust. For more information, visit **ttouch.com**.

Think about this practice in human terms. Humans use mindful methods—such as taking deep breaths—when we need to collect our thoughts.

When we concentrate on breathing, our mind is focused and cannot wander. This melts away stress and other distractions that prevent us from thinking clearly. The TTouch has a similar effect.

Because we can't ask our dogs to take deep breaths or practice other mindful techniques, the TTouches accomplish this for them.

When calm, your dog will learn faster, recover from injury more quickly, and connect with you on a deeper level.

A dog who feels comfortable and balanced in her body is more confident. This feeling of safety gives your dog a better sense of self-control. The results of such a simple shift are incredible!

Confident, emotionally balanced dogs have better decision-making skills. They are less reactive and, therefore, less likely to show aggressive behavior.

This unique approach is widely accepted as a powerful way to improve your dog's behavior and wellbeing. By using it, you will encourage your dog's willingness and ability to learn.

TTouches are a great way to enhance the 1 Minute Dog Training system.

Action Items

- Practice TTouches on your dog. It's okay if you feel inexperienced at first! Just making gentle physical contact with your dog is an excellent start.

- Pay attention to your dog's body language as you explore TTouches together. Follow your dog's signals and your intuition to guide the movement.

- Stay focused and breathe as you practice the TTouches on your dog. This can strengthen your bond and prove to be meaningful time spent together.

Let's Review

- TTouches may calm your dog, help with pain management, anxiety, training puppies, car sickness, and confidence.

- You can do TTouches all over the body, or you can focus on one area. Working different parts of your dog's anatomy will have a unique effect.

- TTouches are also a fantastic reward for a job well done.

- Practicing these touches creates a very special bond, both physically and mentally.

CHAPTER EIGHT
OUR RELATIONSHIP WITH DOGS

Let's dive into the foundation of the 1 Minute Dog Training concept.

For many people, having a relationship with their dog is natural—it is why they have a dog in the first place. They love their dog.

I know a lot of dog lovers who take their pup everywhere they go. Some even sleep with their dog!

Others see dogs as "friendly wolves."

This is understandable, as UCLA Professor of Ecology and Evolutionary Biology Robert Wayne has proven that a dog's DNA matches the gray wolf's by 99%.[3]

Many well-regarded celebrity trainers say your dog thinks they are part of a wolf pack. They claim that unless you are the dominant "Alpha," your dog will never listen. Numerous studies have shown that this idea promotes abusive training.[4]

NOT ONLY IS THE ALPHA DOG APPROACH CRUEL, BUT THE LOGIC BEHIND IT IS ALSO DEEPLY FLAWED.

I feel very certain that dogs recognize us as humans, and not wolves or dogs. So, there is no reason to behave like we are members of a wolf pack.

I have worked with both wolves and dogs. I can assure you that dogs and wolves are different animals.

I have worked with Gray Wolves, Red Wolves, and wolf puppies. I have also helped train hybrid Wolfdogs, the offspring of a wolf and a dog.

You would think that wolves are just like dogs because they resemble dogs. But wolves are wild animals. Their bite cracks bones. While a few people have successfully raised wolves, almost all fail.[5]

I can assure you that, even as puppies, wolves or hybrid Wolfdog puppies are not the same as a Golden Retriever.

I once worked with a wolf pack in New Mexico. When I looked at the young wolf pups, they had an untamed sense. Almost all of them cautiously stood back.

When I could get close enough to look into their eyes, there was a wildness, a fierceness that reflects tens of thousands of years of separate evolutions. In all my experience with dogs, this was a trait I had never seen.

If I moved toward the wolf puppies, they would growl. You would think that wolves are just like dogs because they resemble dogs. But they are wild animals. They are wolves.

To better understand this difference, let's explore a human example.

Since researchers sequenced the chimpanzees' DNA, we have known that humans share about 99% of our DNA with chimps.[6] This makes them our closest living relatives; chimps are to us what wolves are to dogs.

Chimps also have an Alpha male in their tribe.[7] We, however, have hopefully evolved past this.

We are not chimpanzees, even though we share most of our DNA with them. Treating our dogs like their wild ancestors makes as much sense as treating people like apes.

So how did we get here? Let's go back in time a bit. Over 30,000 years ago, when early hunters became friends with an animal: The wolf.

Can't you picture it? Our human ancestors are in a cave, huddled around a fire. Out of the dark, someone brings in a wolf puppy.

People jump back, astonished. The puppy whines. Cautiously—eyes wide—someone throws a piece of meat from the fire at the future of dogs.

Some wolves were bred, and they changed as we fed and cared for them. Over time, they developed smaller brains, smaller paws, and smaller teeth. We don't need a scientist to tell us that their ears drooped.

They became the dogs that we know and love today. And there are now about 900,000,000 dogs with whom we share our planet.

The idea that we must dominate our dogs and treat them like wolves is very bizarre to me.

As most dog owners know, dogs have a passionate kinship with humans. However, wolves do not. The relationship we formed with our dogs is what created our furry best friends.

Almost everyone who has a dog loves them deeply, and new evidence strongly supports that the feeling is mutual.

One MRI study examined which part of dogs' brains lights up when they hear their owner's voice. The same part of the human brain lights up when we love someone or something.[8] This shows that our dogs really love us too!

If you weren't already convinced that we should treat our dogs like they are our friends instead of wolves, then consider this:

> **WHY WOULD WE YELL AT, HIT, CHOKE, OR ABUSE AN ANIMAL THAT LOVES US?**

If you're still not persuaded, another team of researchers found interesting evidence explaining the behavioral differences between dogs and wolves. The researchers found a fascinating gene in the DNA of dogs.

The main trait of this gene is extreme friendliness. One theory is that we selectively bred dogs to be friendly.

This practice passed this "friendly" gene from one dog to the next. The result is the affectionate animals we know and love today.

Selective breeding in favor of a friendly personality quickly created behavioral differences between dogs and wolves.[9]

They have been very different animals for thousands of years. Let's treat them like they are dogs, not wolves!

MANY PEOPLE PRACTICE THE ALPHA DOG METHOD SIMPLY BECAUSE THEY DO NOT KNOW BETTER. THEY MAY HAVE LEARNED THAT DOGS ONLY RESPOND TO DOMINANCE TRAINING.

SOME EVEN FIND THAT CHOKING A DOG IS EASIER THAN TAKING THE TIME TO TRAIN WITH PATIENCE.

IF YOU WANT TO "ALPHA" YOUR DOG, PLENTY OF BOOKS WILL TEACH YOU HOW TO SHOCK, CHOKE, COMMAND, AND PUNISH THEM.

THERE IS ANOTHER WAY THAT I STRONGLY ENCOURAGE YOU TO FOLLOW, WHICH INVITES YOU TO TRAIN WITH COMPASSIONATE LEADERSHIP AND GUIDANCE.

I know it's not always easy. I have even tried to rush my dog when taking her outside to the bathroom.

I will be the first to admit that I have struggled to train a dog.

I've even thought, "All I need to do is put a shock, pinch or choke collar on this guy, and he will listen to me."

But thankfully, as is necessary for all relationships, I worked past my frustration, and so can you!

The results have been a win for both my dog and me. It places us in a relationship rather than a power struggle. Studies have shown again and again that dominance training can be dangerous.

A study in Science Daily proved that "dominated dogs" tend to be much more aggressive towards their owners and, more importantly, towards children.[10]

My own experience combined with this data, shows that the relationships between dogs and humans form through understanding and conscious leadership.

As always, training our dogs with patience, consistency, and affection is the best way!

Let's Review

- Your dog is a dog, not a wolf.

- Don't "alpha" your dog! Form a relationship built on mutual trust and love.

- Our relationship with dogs has lasted tens of thousands of years. For many of us, dogs are truly our best friends.

- Dogs who are trained with aggressive methods are much more likely to be aggressive - especially toward children.

- Lead your dog with patience and kindness!

CHAPTER NINE
LEASH TRAINING WITH COMPASSION

This is how many trainers tell you to make your dog listen when walking on a leash:

"Put a chain around their neck. If they don't listen, choke them. Then, with a one-word command, tell them what you want."

Can we agree that there might be a better way? You can train your dog to walk on a leash and strengthen your bond in the same 1 minute session.

I once worked with a 2-year-old dog named Sheba. She refused to walk on a leash without pulling, jerking, and going in any direction she wanted.

Sheba's human guardians had tried harnesses, flat collars, chain choke collars, and finally went to pinch collars. The couple, Matt and Lisa, were husband and wife.

To some degree, this dog was their only child. They had raised her since she was a puppy.

The couple loved their dog. They brought her to me because she would lunge and leap at other dogs every time they went to the dog park.

She was not aggressive. She just wanted to get off the leash to play.

When they let her off the leash at the dog park, it would sometimes take over an hour to get her back.

She would run away in a playful way when they would try to catch her, and she would not come when called.

Whenever Sheba had pulled on the leash or when she did not listen, she was aggressively disciplined. Sheba had learned to associate Matt and Lisa's voices with pain. Why would she want to listen or come when called?

First, I asked Sheba's guardians to describe what they wanted out of their relationship with their dog.

The goal was to help them understand why Sheba acted the way she did.

The husband, Matt, said Sheba did whatever she wanted to do. The wife, Lisa, said she was sweet and just needed more training.

I told them they were both right. Sheba needed conscious training, and then the stubbornness and the running away would become a thing of the past. They both looked a little skeptical.

We left their home and headed to the dog park. I put a flat collar and a halter on Sheba and attached one snap to the collar and one to the halter. I intended to utilize a harness when walking Sheba after the initial training session.

I also used a 3-foot bamboo wand so I could practice three different kinds of cues when showing Sheba's family how to train her. You could also use a 3-foot piece of bamboo or dowel rod.

Just to be clear, I never use this tool for any type of correction or punishment. It is simply to give a visual cue as an extension of my hand.

I used:

1. A gentle signal on the collar and harness at the same time, using a leash with two attachment points.
2. My voice.
3. I only used the bamboo wand as a visual cue in front of her. Please see your free video for instructions on how to do this at **1minutedog.com**.

I also attached a 15-foot lead to her collar in case she broke free.

We started with the basics to show Sheba what sit, stay, and come meant. Considering she was more resistant to coming when the husband called, as he had disciplined Sheba in the past, Lisa and I stayed with Sheba while Matt walked 10 feet away.

Matt had a treat in hand, which Sheba usually responded to. We also used soothing voice and gentle touch to ground her in the present moment.

Matt held up the treat and called to Sheba. "Sheba! Sheba come. Come here, Sheba! Sheeeba," he called her again and again.

I stopped him and said:

> **"Matt, it's no good if we need to call our dogs a bunch of times. You want her to come when you call the first time."**

This took a few moments to sink in, but I saw in his eyes when he understood our goal.

We started over and used TTouches to regain Sheba's focus. Then, Matt held up the treat and called Sheba while Lisa and I nudged Sheba towards him.

Matt had the 15-foot lead in his hand so that Sheba couldn't run away. She enthusiastically ran toward Matt to get the treat, and he gave it to her.

But Matt forgot to have Sheba sit before she got the treat. So, we started over and followed all the same steps. When she went to Matt this time, he asked her to sit, which she did not do.

He told her, "Sit! Sheba, sit" again and again. I walked up to Matt and said, "Hey, do you remember what I said about calling her once?" This time, Matt smiled and got it right away.

So, we went back and did it again. When she came to get the treat, Matt said, "Sheba, please sit."

We helped her into a seated position before she got her reward. This whole process took maybe three or four minutes.

We took a break for a couple of minutes and kept Sheba on a leash. Because I was paid by the hour, we repeated this process many times before our hour was up.

LEASH TRAINING WITH COMPASSION

After, Matt and Lisa were very diligent about practicing these micro sessions at home. They also replaced treats with physical affection and praise early on.

I only had two more sessions with them after the original one. They said they were amazed by how well Sheba was listening.

The last time I worked with Sheba at the dog park, about two weeks after our first session, we were able to ask Sheba to sit, stay, and wait while all three of us walked 50 feet away.

We counted to ten, called her, and she bounded over to us and waited for her affectionate reward.

In that same session, we started working with Sheba on the leash. Because we had practiced the sit, stay, and come initially, she was very willing to learn. These skills are the foundation of all others.

Dogs are smart! They want to make us happy, even when they aren't treated with the kindness they deserve.

When I left Sheba, Lisa, and Matt at the park, Sheba was walking next to them slowly and paying close attention—even as countless other dogs ran around.

Action Items

- Start with techniques mentioned in the story above. Both you and your dog will enjoy your walks together in no time!

- The key is to review your dog's sit, stay, and come skills.

- If your dog can reliably sit, stay, and come, she is ready to learn to walk on a leash without pulling.

LEASH TRAINING WITH COMPASSION

- 🐾 The right equipment will really help with leash training.

- 🐾 Sit, stay, and come are the foundation of leash training.

- 🐾 You do not need a shock, choke, or pinch collar to train your dog how to walk on a leash.

- 🐾 When you ask your dog to do something, give her time to figure it out. Say it once, then wait and see what she does.

- 🐾 Remember to use a variety of clues (visual, verbal, and physical *gentle touch*) when training your dog.

CHAPTER TEN
WHY DO DOGS PULL ON A LEASH?

"Dogs are our link to paradise. To sit with a dog on a hillside on a glorious afternoon is to be back in Eden, where doing nothing was not boring—it was peace."

- Milan Kundera

Let's think about this from your pup's point of view:

Dogs mainly interact with the outside world when tethered to a leash. That's usually about 5 feet of freedom.

For many dogs, going for a walk is like a child going to Disney World.

Sure, it is necessary to take your dog outside, especially if he needs to take care of business. But from your dog's perspective, it is more than simply finding a spot to go potty. It may be the most exciting part of his day!

WHY DO DOGS PULL ON A LEASH?

I have taken dogs outside thousands of times to go for a walk, go potty or play. Usually, it is a combination of all three things.

Regardless, the excitement, eagerness, and tail-wagging are constantly there.

So, how do you stop leash pulling and make the experience fun for you both? It doesn't matter if you are starting with a young puppy or working with an older dog.

Begin with the three training basics:

- Sit
- Stay
- Come

It is essential to practice walking on a leash with your dog inside the house before going outside.

In my experience, leash training will be more challenging if you try going directly outside with all the related smells and distractions.

Remember to use your hand signals, the right collar, harness or head collar, and a calm voice.

Many people use clickers to get their dog's attention. I choose not to use clickers because I think the sound of my voice is more effective. And I may not always have a clicker with me. Instead, I generally use a subtle sound such as a "cluck."

As you begin leash training, you may find it helpful to use treats. But you want to phase out treats early as your dog's skills improve.

Replace the treats with praise, TTouches and love. This way, your dog pays attention because they want to listen, not because they think you have something tasty.

I have seen many dogs who only listen or come when called because they think they will get a treat. In the long run, it is better that your dog comes when called because she *wants* to, not just because she wants a treat.

The reward system of touch and praise will deepen your relationship with your dog as you learn together.

As with all 1 Minute Dog Training, it is best to practice leash training regularly in short sessions.

If you'd like, you can check out the leash training video on **1minutedog.com** and see what one of my leash training sessions looks like.

You will need a leash or piece of rope at least 10 feet long. For these sessions, please do not use retractable leashes.

Please see Roxy waiting at the end of her long line leash as we practice indoors.

Leash Training:
Step-by-step session

Make sure you have been practicing **sit**, **stay**, and **come** in 1-2 minute sessions.

In this session, you will modify this to **sit**, **wait**, and **walk**. Here is how to do this:

1. Staying inside the house, walk around with your dog on a leash, keeping her next to you. The goal is to keep the leash loose.
2. Ask your dog to sit and wait. Take several breaths. Then, Repeat the walk exercise slowly. Occasionally stop, ask your dog to sit and wait, and drop the leash beside you.
3. When your dog sits and waits, praise her thoroughly.

Continue to cycle through sit, wait, and walk with your dog next to you while still inside the house. This is the first step to leash training your dog effectively.

You are simply teaching your dog to listen and walk next to you. I find this is the most productive way to prevent leash pulling and other behavioral challenges too!

While I am doing this, with many dogs, I speak to them in full sentences and explain what I am doing.

I might say something like, "Max, this is leash training. This is really important for both of us to understand, so we can go many places together."

There is another exercise you might try inside the house. I call this "Walking Concentration.' At first, practice this with the leash on. It is a very effective form of training.

In many cases, it will help with leash training your dog much faster. Once you and your dog become more proficient, try this without the leash.

WALKING CONCENTRATION: Step-by-step session

1. Have your dog stand or sit next to you. Politely ask him to stay.
2. Take one step and stop.
3. Have your dog do the same, and then sit down.
4. Look down and praise your dog.
5. Take another step and pause.
6. Do this about ten times and slightly increase the length of the pause.

Many people tend to hold their breath while doing this, so remember to breathe.

This simple exercise in 1 minute segments can make a lasting difference in your relationship with your dog.

Once your dog comfortably walks next to you inside the house with a slack leash, it's time to head outside.

Before you go out, you may want to tell your dog what you will do, such as, "Are you ready to go outside?"

Remember, it's meaningful to speak in complete sentences rather than one-word commands, as you would in any relationship.

Before you go outside, it's worth reviewing that the most important part of this process is that your dog will come when called. Please make sure you have successfully worked with this inside your house.

Remember, you want your dog to consistently come when called, whether he on a leash or not.

WHY DO DOGS PULL ON A LEASH?

**Your dog should come to you
because he genuinely wants to be with you.**

When I am out walking our dog (and a car is coming toward us), I have a habit of telling her, "A car is coming. Please come back and sit next to me," even if she is on a leash.

She loves this exercise because she knows she will always get praise for coming back to me.

One way to ensure your dog always wants to be near you is by being kind. I know that is easier said than done.

Speaking from experience, kindness sometimes takes a backseat to frustration.

I was recently swimming with our dog, Roxy. She's a Belgian Malinois with high energy and, by nature, wants to take care of everyone.

Her instinct is to always look out for people in trouble. While she cares deeply for our family, she's also highly driven to protect everyone.

While we were swimming together just offshore in the ocean, some children played nearby. One child started screaming out of joy as he splashed around.

Roxy instantly switched into lifeguard mode and darted towards the child she thought was in danger.

Her good-natured impulse propelled her right across my body. Her claws snagged on my arm as she rapidly swam to the child.

I was in pain (not to mention we were quite a ways offshore) and bleeding quite a bit.

Thankfully, if my injury attracted any nearby sharks, I was oblivious to their presence. Still, I was upset.

I knew Roxy did this out of concern for a child, but I was in pain and reacted by pushing her away from me with a fair bit of force.

Then, I took a minute to collect myself. In an instant, I remembered the fear of being attacked.

Roxy is the farthest thing from an aggressive dog, yet I felt genuinely scared. I was shocked.

It's hard to be kind when your dog isn't listening. It's even more difficult when that frustration is coupled with concern for your well-being.

I am not perfect. I struggle to stay calm at times. But despite that, I choose to let these moments shape my relationship with Roxy.

Consider your dog's intentions and your own. Examine your emotions. Are you feeling angry at your dog? Does she deserve that?

It might feel easier to redirect that anger and take it out on your dog. Maybe you are angry at the situation, someone else, or another dog.

You get to choose how you react. You could let your anger take over, or you can regain control of the situation.

I recommend taking a few deep breaths. Ask yourself: What kind of dog guardian do I want to be?

Whether your dog scratches you in the ocean or pulls on the leash, you can always choose wisdom and patience.

If you've let your frustration win in the past, it's okay. I can assure you that I have too. We can all be more mindful.

Action Items

- Review sit, stay, and come for 1 minute with your dog.

- Practice leash training with your dog inside your house before practicing outside.

- Remember that a walk might be the best part of your dog's whole day! It is normal for dogs to get so excited that they forget their good manners.

- Be patient and consistent as you work on this very important skill.

WHY DO DOGS PULL ON A LEASH?

Let's Review

- Remind yourself that walks are probably the best part of your dog's day! Be patient and let them explore.

- Leash training begins with sit, stay, and come.

- Practice walking your dog on a leash inside before you go outside.

- Do your best to stay calm when your dog doesn't listen.

CHAPTER ELEVEN
WHY YOU SHOULD NEVER CHOKE YOUR DOG

When you choke a dog, they will become afraid and, in some cases, aggressive. If so, that can be dangerous.

Not to mention that restricting your dog's ability to breathe is cruel and life-threatening.

Am I saying that choking your dog doesn't work? No, it might work—but it comes at a price.

If you use dominance training, you may get a dog who listens out of fear. But you may also end up with a dog so traumatized or afraid that they will not listen, and their natural goodness is repressed.

> **I KNOW OF MANY DOGS THAT HAVE BECOME AGGRESSIVE, UNPREDICTABLE, AND DANGEROUS THROUGH CRUEL TRAINING METHODS. THESE DOGS MAY BE ESPECIALLY AGGRESSIVE TOWARDS CHILDREN.**

It's been tens of thousands of years since we domesticated dogs. Surely that is enough time for us to understand our dogs and train them in a kinder, more effective way.

WHY YOU SHOULD NEVER CHOKE YOUR DOG

Imagine if your boss used a choke collar on you. Instead of simply asking you to do something, how would you feel if they barked one-word commands and choked you?

You'd probably quit that job! Or, at the very least, you wouldn't like your boss. And you'd most likely hate going to work every day.

You want your dog to enjoy the time you spend together. You want her to listen because she wants to. Treating your dog with respect is the first step toward establishing a great relationship.

When walking and leash training your dog, a harness + a collar is much better than a collar alone. The harness + collar combination allows you to give your dog signals on the lead without choking her.

Here is how I attach a two point lead to Roxy's collar and harness.

Roxy is very comfortable, safe, and balanced on the leash this way.

CHAPTER TWELVE
CHAIN, PRONG AND SHOCK COLLARS

Many trainers will tell you that a properly fitted chain choke collar is the easiest way to train your dog. In my experience, this is not true.

Choke collars

A choke collar allows a person to give the dog what is commonly called a "correction," which is a painful snap and release on the choke chain collar.

Some trainers claim that you can stop unwanted behavior by taking the dog's attention away from what they are doing. Supposedly, this makes the dog behave calmly again. They say all you need to know is how to use them properly.

CHAIN, PRONG AND SHOCK COLLARS

The problem is that choke collars are innately cruel, and it is very easy to misuse them.

This is particularly true if kids regularly walk the dog. Children are more prone to misuse or overuse of the chain, which can hurt or frighten the dog.

Prong collars

You might have also heard that a prong collar is the most civilized and harmless way to train a dog. In my opinion, this is entirely untrue.

I feel, as do many trainers, that prong/spike collars are even worse than chain choke collars.

Prong collars have spikes that stab a dog's neck every time the leash is jerked, and the collar is used as a "correction."

Even without a jerking motion, these collars can still cause pain, injury, and, in extreme cases, lifelong damage.

Shock Collars

The use of electronic shock collars is a highly emotional topic.

Many trainers will say, "Shock collars will stop your dog from running out into the road and getting hit by a car."

They promise only to use it on vibrate or the lowest shock settings. Most people use shock collars because they either don't know what else to do or, in my opinion, do not want to take the time to properly train their dog.

I know a lovely dog that was trained with a shock collar. She's terrific, but now her owners can't get her to stop barking—even when shocked.

When they go to pet her head, she shies away. I have seen this happen to many dogs who have become victims of dog trainers in an unregulated industry.

In my opinion, there are always risks with adverse training, and the possibility of permanent damage or long-term trauma is likely.

As you can see in the photo below, there are two prongs that rest against the dog's neck. These prongs transmit a painful electric shock directly onto the dog's sensitive neck. The blue arrow is pointing to the prongs for your convenience.

If you have questions about this, please speak with your veterinarian and read on.

According to a study published in the Journal of Applied Animal Welfare Science by Richard Polsky, dogs in shock containment systems (for example, within an invisible or underground fence) may express extreme aggression towards humans.

Polsky also found that electronic shock collars work only a small percentage of the time. They teach dogs to be afraid of both people and the collar itself.[11]

In October 2020, Petco made a brilliant decision with other online retailers to stop carrying electronic shock collars.

Why? Because they realized this method was cruel. Petco's CEO stated:

"Electricity may be critical to powering your microwave, but it has no role for the average pet parent training their dog," said Ron Coughlin, CEO of the San Diego-based company.

Dr. Whitney Miller, head of veterinary medicine for Petco, followed this statement. She said:

"Science shows animals will learn a new behavior faster and more successfully if they are allowed to voluntarily participate in the learning process and are rewarded for preferred behaviors. Punishment is not only less successful in changing unwanted behaviors, shock collars have been known to actually reinforce negative behaviors and create anxiety within pets."

Continuing with this movement, Alexandra Horowitz, MS, Ph.D., author of the #1 New York Times bestseller *Inside of a Dog*, senior research fellow, and head of the Horowitz Dog Cognition Lab at Barnard College said:

"Shock collars are misguided, antiquated, harmful equipment. It's great to see Petco taking the lead in removing this merchandise from their stores in support of their advocacy of positive reinforcement training."

Last, a recent Edelman Intelligence online survey reported that 70 percent of dog owners feel that shock collars harm their pet's emotional or mental well-being. In fact, 59 percent of dog owners who participated in the study said they would rather shock themselves than use a shock collar on their dogs.[12]

As a last word from me on the subject, Australia has admirably banned the use of electronic shock collars and made it illegal to import prong or pinch collars into the country.

Instead of using a prong, shock, or choke collar, there are many safe and ethical alternatives I recommend. Please visit **1minutedog.com** to see which products I use with my own dog.

If you're looking for more information on how to take full advantage of these helpful training tools, please visit **1minutedog.com** to watch your FREE training videos. It includes a video where I discuss my favorite equipment and demonstrate how I use it.

CHAIN, PRONG AND SHOCK COLLARS

Now that you know which tools to use and how to use them, you are ready to walk your dog with confidence. It's time to go outside and practice walking your dog on a leash!

Before you venture into a neighborhood where there may be other dogs and plenty of distractions, practice leash training inside your house before moving into your yard.

Once you feel comfortable in your yard, you can move further out into other areas.

Let's Review

- Choke chains, prongs, and shock collars are painful and outdated training tools.

- Abusive training methods tend to make dogs more fearful and therefore aggressive.

- All modern research has shown that using pain and fear to train dogs is cruel and unnecessary.

CHAPTER THIRTEEN
IS YOUR DOG SMART?

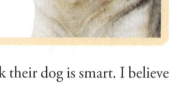

What did the dog say after he jumped on his owner and got her muddy?

"Please fur-give me."

People frequently ask me if I think their dog is smart. I believe dogs are like people—some are smarter than others.

It really comes down to how you define intelligence. If a dog has a long history of abuse or time in a rescue shelter, it may take more patience and training to reach his full potential.

I think dogs are generally more intelligent than we give them credit for.

I heard a story about an 18-month-old pup who jumped a 5-foot fence to get out of the yard on the 4th of July. The dog was spooked when the neighbors set off fireworks.

The people that lived with this dog spent most of the night looking for her. They finally gave up at midnight after walking many miles and driving all over the neighborhood.

They went to sleep heartbroken, thinking they would never see her again. But, at 3:00 AM, their doorbell rang. They had a video camera at their door.

When they went to see who rang the bell, who did they see? It was their dog! She had gone into hiding because of the fireworks and then came home after they were over. And amazingly, she rang the doorbell to tell them she was back.

The funny thing is the family could not recall that their dog had ever actually seen the doorbell ring. They weren't sure how she knew to ring the bell. That seems super smart to me.

I think most animals are smarter than we give them credit for. They just usually have a very different way of thinking than we do.

We have a family cat named Dash. We abide by a very regular feeding routine with our animals. Dash always knows what to expect, and he loves the consistency of it.

Not long ago, my wife Samara filled Dash's bowl with his favorite chicken dinner and placed the bowl on the ground.

She put the bowl about ten feet away from where it usually is because it was raining. She figured Dash would quickly chow down on his favorite meal.

He looked at the bowl full of fresh, fragrant food and just walked away. He had absolutely no interest in it. So, she picked up the dish, waited a few minutes for him to work up his appetite, and tried again.

We placed the bowl where it had just been, only a little away from its regular spot. We waited to see what Dash would do this time.

He looked at the bowl and then up at me. He wouldn't even touch his food!

I finally slid his dish over to its usual place. Dash immediately dug in. He gleefully munched down his entire meal, so I knew he was hungry the whole time.

So what happened? This got me thinking about how each creature's brain is wired differently.

Every living thing has a brain that works a certain way. It is challenging to understand the complexities of an animal's mind. We can't just ask them what they're thinking!

In Dash's brain, mealtime is a precise process. It's the way things have always been. Even the slightest adjustment threw a wrench in the whole thing.

Each cat thinks uniquely, and cats think differently than dogs. But most animals love routine. They feel safe and comfortable when they know exactly what to expect.

And that's why it is so important to train your dog consistently. Daily 1 minute sessions will produce better long-term results than longer intermittent sessions.

On the flip side of that coin, animals can be consistent to a fault. Most people who share their homes with pets have experienced this.

When you want your dog to do something, it can be frustrating if he doesn't listen.

But chances are, your dog isn't trying to be naughty. He might just be thinking, "but that's not the way we do it." It can be difficult to figure out what's causing your dog's defiance.

Consider it a wonderful opportunity to practice empathy.

You can always go back to the basics. Build off what your dog confidently understands. Use sit, stay, and come as a springboard for all other behaviors. You'd be surprised at how well this works!

In some ways, dogs are even more intelligent than people. They have incredible abilities that no human has. If you were to look at the world through your dog's eyes, things would be very different.

While humans have superior vision and taste, our hearing and ability to smell hardly compare to our dogs'. They have incredibly resourceful noses and can hear far better than we can.

Not only do dogs interact with the world in a different way than we do, but they use their unique talents to help us. Dogs do some of the most meaningful jobs in the world.

From finding people trapped under rubble to performing water rescues and sniffing out everything from cancer[13] to dangerous explosives, dogs are true heroes.

Our dogs easily outperform us in scent and hearing. Even more incredible is that dogs are equipped with a sixth sense: internal GPS.

Part of this ability comes from dogs' superior sniffers. And part of it has to do with dogs' sensitivity to Earth's magnetic field. Dogs basically have an internal compass.[14]

There are countless stories about dogs beating all odds and finding their way back to their humans.

I recently read a story about a 10-month-old puppy who jumped overboard while boating with her family in Michigan.

The couple had gone down below deck to work on the engine and left her up on the main deck. When they came back up after making the repair, their dog was gone.

Image Copyright © Time.com

They drove their boat around the lake for hours in search of her. The family knew she could swim for an hour or two, but after four hours of desperate searching, they started to feel hopeless.

They radioed all the nearby boats but were unsure if anyone had heard their call. As the sun began to set, the temperature dropped.

The family's chances of finding their pup—especially in the water—were shrinking every minute.

But they never gave up.

The next day, the family hiked through the forest from their house towards where they had moored their boat. They were hopeful as they constantly squeaked their puppy's favorite toy.

They heard a rustle nearby. They called her name and looked all around. They couldn't believe their eyes when their puppy came bounding towards them from behind the trees! Tears filled their eyes as they kneeled to the ground, hugging her as she licked their faces.

They quickly realized their ten-month-old puppy swam six miles to shore. Even more incredible, she hiked twelve miles through dense forest before they were reunited.

And this dog was only a puppy! Most grown adults wouldn't be able to find their way home from 18 miles away, even with a GPS.

I think it goes without saying that dogs are smart. They can pull off the most remarkable stunts. And yet, they are so humble.

They use their abilities to guide the blind, give courage to our most vulnerable, and comfort those who suffer. Most dogs love children unconditionally and energize the elderly.

As a small token of my appreciation for our incredible service dogs, a percentage of this book's proceeds will be donated to Guide Dogs for the Blind and other shelter dogs. These nonprofits provide children and adults who have disabilities with trained service dogs.

These organizations increase the quality of life for people with special needs, and also teach valuable lessons about confidence and independence. I encourage you to check out **1minutedog.com** to find out more information on how you can donate to his foundation if you feel compelled.

All animals are different, and their unique skills are difficult to compare. As we have established, dogs are very intelligent creatures.

Dolphins, however, are generally considered the smartest marine animal. They are also trained, similar to the way dogs are. And what methods do these trainers use? They use positive reinforcement!

This means that the dolphins are never punished. Instead, they are rewarded for good behavior. Their skills are shaped through a system of rewards.

Research shows that both dolphins and dogs are too smart to be unnecessarily dominated! They are intelligent enough to be led with patience and kindness—enthusiastic encouragement is all they need to succeed.

IS YOUR DOG SMART?

My daughter Malia working at Dolphin Quest Hawaii.

Visit **dolphinquest.com** to read nore abour their humane treatment of sea animals!

Did You Know?

Dolphins are extremely intelligent and the smartest marine animals.

Dogs and dolphins are both playful, social, and smart!

Dolphins are only trained using positive reinforcement.

Research has proven that animals respond best to positive reinforcement.

Science says it's the best way to train your dog!

CHAPTER FOURTEEN
THE DOG'S BRAIN

"Dogs do speak, but only to those who know how to listen."

- Orhan Pamuk

Many studies have researched the dog's brain. It was quickly discovered that the dog's mind has much more brain power than many other animals.

MRI studies have proven that dogs can experience emotions like joy, depression, anxiety, and even post-traumatic stress disorder (PTSD).[15]

Some dogs, particularly rescue dogs and military and police service dogs, have been diagnosed with PTSD and put on various anti-anxiety medications, which are effective.

Some people think dogs can't make plans. But anybody who's been around a dog knows that they clearly understand when it's time for dinner. In my book, that qualifies as making plans. I've seen it over and over again.

My dog knows when it's time for breakfast or dinner. She *absolutely* knows when it's 5 o'clock and time to go for a walk or go out and play. She also knows when to check whether the cat has finished his food or left any scraps behind.

Another fascinating thing is that dogs dream! What does it mean when they are whimpering, their feet are moving, or they are barking in their dreams?

Scientists suggest that, because their brains are complex, they dream about experiences from the recent past.[16]

I have watched dogs dream hundreds of times. I still smile when our dog starts to whimper, her paws start to run, or she starts to bark while dreaming.

I always wonder what is happening when she growls while she's dreaming.

How intelligent are dogs? It's been proposed that they can process a lot of information because they have so many neurons in their brains.

Dogs can recognize different people and identify various facial emotions and visual cues. They use these to guide their interactions with you.[17]

For example, let's say your couch is an off-limits place for your dog. If you came home one day and found that the couch was warm and covered in dog hair, you may raise an eyebrow and look at your dog.

Your dog will probably understand exactly what that facial expression means and respond with her own signature look.

In 2017, Time magazine wrote a fascinating article after studying a dog's brain under an MRI machine. The researcher discovered that dogs likely experience certain aspects of the world similar to us.[18]

Although there is no way to tell for sure, the researcher strongly believes this to be true after watching dogs' brain scans in response to various stimuli.

There's no doubt, at least in my mind, that dogs unmistakably experience joy. When my daughters come home from school, our dog spins, yips, and has more joy than any human I know.

It's also been shown in experiments with closed circuit cameras that dogs know when their humans are coming home. They start checking the front door or become restless and excited long before their family returns home.[19]

Is this intuition, a function of their brain, or do they have some sense that connects them to us on a deeper level than we understand?

THE DOG'S BRAIN

- Dogs have very complex brains. They can experience powerful emotions!

- If you've ever seen a dog dream, then you know their minds are constantly at work.

- Dogs can also recognize a variety of facial expressions. They use these visual cues to better understand us.

CHAPTER FIFTEEN
YOUR DOG'S NAME

What's in a dog's name? Plenty. And yet, many dogs think their names are "no," "stop," or "sit" because their owners say it over and over again. Wouldn't you think the same?

The name we give a dog is important. A dog is a family member; as such, naming them should be given consideration and care.

Can you rename your dog? Sure, this is common for families who adopt a rescue with a name they do not like. This should especially be done if the name they came with evokes a negative emotion.

Am I suggesting that you should change your dog's name? In most cases, the answer would be no.

In some instances, where the dog's name seems unsuitable, of course, you can change your dog's name. I think it should be a group decision if you have a family.

You could also ask your dog how they feel about a new name. You can see what reactions you get when you give them options. You should also see what emotions come up for you with the new name. How does it make you feel?

I once helped change an Australian Shepherd puppy's name from Scratchy to Scooby.

In that training session, we discussed how Scratchy had a habit of jumping up on people and the bed. He would scratch and paw at his family to get what he wanted.

Once they changed the dog's name—and, more importantly—worked with the 1 Minute Dog system, that behavior stopped. Names are meaningful, not only for dogs but for other animals as well.

I worked with a celebrity in the San Francisco Bay Area years ago. This celebrity and his partner called me to help them understand why their cats were fighting.

They had seven cats in total, and all lived together in peace. All, that is, but two.

One was a large gray cat; the other was tiny and black. During our first meeting, I sat down with the clients and their two cats.

The cats seemed to tolerate each other, but they clearly weren't friends. I asked the clients what exactly happened when they fought.

They said they would be fine for a while, and then out of nowhere, they would start to circle each other and hiss.

I watched them for a minute or so before asking their names. "The gray one is Bronson," the celebrity said, "and the black one is Eastwood."

For those of you who didn't grow up in the '80s, Clint Eastwood and Charles Bronson were world-renowned Hollywood actors best known for facing off in western gunfights.

Am I saying the only reason these cats fought was because of their names? No. But I felt then, as I feel now, that it contributed to the tension between them.

The tone of voice we use to call our pet's names can make a huge difference in how they react—as do their very names.

Ultimately, Bronson and Eastwood stopped behaving like they were in a Western corral, ready for battle.

The couple actually sat down and had a conversation with both cats. They asked them to please get along and have peace in their household.

They were also aware of when it seemed like the cats were about to fight. This was when the couple used several techniques, including the TTouch, and these two cats quickly learned to become more accepting of each other.

This is me doing TTouch work on a cat.

Another one of those techniques was intentions, which we will learn next.

CHAPTER SIXTEEN
YOUR INTENTION ROADMAP

You will find training sessions more productive and successful if you spend 1 minute planning what you want to do beforehand.

For example, your goal might be to have a kind, intelligent, well-trained dog you can take anywhere.

It helps to have an intention or a roadmap. These intentions can be small yet significant steps you take in training your dog.

An intention will help you focus on what you hope to accomplish in a 1 minute session. What I mean by "hope" is to earnestly expect that you and your dog will work together in a meaningful way.

You can work on the same intention for five to ten sessions until your dog gets the hang of what you've been practicing.

Go ahead and let your dog know what your intention is. Say it aloud: "Max, we are going to work on sit and stay today." Hold that objective in your mind, and repeatedly share it with your dog.

Also, keep in mind what it will look like when the session is over. Do you see Max sitting and paying attention? Do you see him staying when you walk to another room? Intentions help these images become a reality.

If it's something that you enjoy doing, you can also keep a 1 Minute Dog Journal. This is a great way to log your progress and keep track of your intentions.

While there are no hard rules about setting intentions, to start, I encourage you to pick one of the three main goals of the 1 Minute Dog Training philosophy:

- Sit
- Stay
- Come

You can start with one of the above and then try a combination of two or all three.

If possible, you can also intend to set a regular time for your 1 minute session(s). You could plan to do a 1 minute session first thing in the morning or for 1 minute before dinner.

Interestingly, I find children are better at setting an intention before a 1-minute session than adults—it comes naturally to them.

Intentions make training more straightforward. I think you might agree that having an untrained dog is a mistake. It's unfair for both the pup and their guardian.

I understand life can be busy! I have children, a business, and a full life. When I feel too rushed, I stop and remind myself I have 1 minute. Please remember that consistency is what will make the biggest difference.

We are always busy as humans, but I know we can all spare a minute for our wonderful dogs.

There is no need to have your dog constantly pulling on the leash, barking all night, or always jumping up on people.

We want our dogs to enhance our lives, not make them more difficult! The fun part (practicing daily with your dog) is up to you!

When put into practice, setting an intention will help you develop an extraordinary relationship with your dog. It may seem too easy to be true, but you have everything to gain by giving it a try.

Remember that frequent training sessions will also allow you to develop a more intimate relationship with your dog. By strengthening your bond with your dog, your intentions will likely become clearer.

Working together with your dog towards a common goal is one of the best ways to deeply connect!

Action Items

- Try to set an intention before your next 1 minute training session with your dog.

- It's okay if it feels silly at first - you will get the hang of it!

- As you set your intention, visualize your dog's good behavior and work towards that image.

- Think of intentions as small goals that you set for each training session.

- Share your intention with your dog. Focus on it for the duration of your 1 minute session.

- Picture how your dog will behave after you have worked together on her skills.

- Start with small intentions. These should be a bunch of little wins that add up to substantial success.

CHAPTER SEVENTEEN
NIPPING AND BITING

I am sure you understand by now that I love dogs. But I have been bitten and I know how scary it can be.

To be completely honest, I went back and forth on whether to talk about nipping or biting in this book. It is challenging to give general advice when each dog is different.

In my experience with home visits, I would get to know a family, their home environment, and of course, their dog. Many times, people would call me because of an issue that had recently developed with their dog or another animal.

I would ask the family if anything had recently changed— such as a divorce, a new animal, someone leaving for college, or any other changes that could have occurred.

Unfortunately, I cannot tell anyone what causes their dog to bite someone without understanding their dog's history and circumstances.

If you have concerns about whether your dog is aggressive, particularly towards children, please consult with your local veterinarian before trying any of these techniques.

NIPPING AND BITING

It is always best to get personalized recommendations when dealing with the serious matter of aggression. The 1 Minute Dog Training method does not cure dogs with aggression problems or predatory aggression.

Please ensure you take all reasonable precautions to prevent injury to yourself, your family, your children, and others (including dogs).

With that being said, I ultimately decided to discuss this topic with you. One reason is that dog "aggression" is often misunderstood. It is one of the main reasons that dogs are surrendered to shelters and euthanized.

There are steps you can take to minimize or help prevent biting and aggression, and I think they are worth mentioning.

Aggression is a hot topic. It is also a very sensitive issue. I prefer the term "reactivity" since this word seems more fitting for many dogs labeled as aggressive.

There is a fine line between a fearful dog and a dangerous dog.

Most dogs who lash out with aggressive behavior are reacting to a specific event. One of the most common things I have seen is when a young child tries to take something away from a dog.

For example, if a dog has a stuffed toy or piece of food, he can become fearful of losing this item. A dog with a bone can be like a child who just tasted chocolate ice cream for the first time.

Dogs are frequently reactive at the end of their leash. Like humans, when animals are scared, they have a fight-or-flight response.

Try to understand: If you had a collar around your neck that prevented you from choosing "flight," you would probably opt for "fight." Not to mention that an inability to breathe would only heighten your fear!

It helps to be aware that many dogs bite as a reaction to a scary experience. It's impossible to prevent every frightening encounter, but you can minimize the risks with simple training.

A typical fear response is the tightening of muscles. By doing regular TTouches on your dog, you may be able to help reduce his reaction to stressors.

There are other reasons why a dog might bite. Puppies, for example, are biting machines. They explore the world with their mouths. And there is a lot to be curious about when you're only eight weeks old!

Although puppy bites are painful, the consequences of these bites are typically mild. However, it is essential to get your puppy's biting in check. As her jaw gets stronger, her bites will become much more powerful.

You want to teach your puppy not to bite humans from a very young age.

When puppies are young, they are teething. It's essential to give them things to chew on. Read about the chew-friendly products I recommend on **1minutedog.com**.

One of the first things you want to teach any dog is that you should be able to take anything from their mouth easily.

Some dogs find that holding onto a toy can be a fun game. It's one of the reasons why I'm not a huge fan of playing tug-of-war with dogs.

There is a difference between food, which represents life to a dog in its most primal state, and a toy, which represents fun. You should be able to take anything from your dog's mouth, regardless of what it is.

Rough play and lack of mental stimulation can also make puppy biting worse. The combination of these things is a recipe for disaster. And so many family dogs are raised this way!

It makes you think: Are our dogs truly aggressive, or are we not setting them up for success?

Some dogs have experienced trauma, which has truly made them aggressive. If you have young children, I strongly advise you against bringing these dogs into your home.

Children are by far the most common victims of dog bites. They are also more likely to be severely injured by a bite.[20]

It is crucial to teach any child you meet how to behave around your dog. But it is also necessary to understand when a dog is a threat to your family.

PLEASE SEE YOUR VETERINARIAN OR A PROFESSIONAL POSITIVE DOG TRAINER TO GET SPECIFIC HELP FOR AGGRESSION OR YOUR DOG'S UNIQUE SITUATION.

As mentioned previously, I once worked with an Australian Shepard puppy. His family had named him Scratchy because he would jump, bite, and scratch them in bed each morning.

Scratchy also had a habit of biting and scratching their young son while they would play.

I decided there were a couple of different reasons why Scratchy's biting had gotten out of control:

1. Scratchy was a working dog, so he craved a job. It was in his nature. Australian Shepards are bred to herd cattle and sheep, sometimes running 20 miles a day. He needed the mental stimulation and confidence that comes with having responsibilities. Without a job, he had a lot of pent-up energy. And an under-stimulated pup explodes when it's playtime. Which brings me to my next point...

2. The young son would roughhouse with Scratchy. This would get him extra riled up and make the biting much harder to control.

In a free video included in your gift, you will see how we encouraged Scratchy to come when called by making it exciting to be near us.

Just after the video ended, we determined Scratchy's problems, talked about his habits, and showed his family how to train him using the 1 Minute Dog Training method.

Scratchy's guardians also decided to change his name to Scooby and provided him with the outdoor exercise and stimulation he needed.

NIPPING AND BITING

Let's Review

- If you fear that your dog is dangerous, please consult with your veterinarian.

- Aggression is often misunderstood. Many dogs are simply afraid.

- A dog's ability to react appropriately to an event is compromised when he is on a leash.

- Practice extreme caution when your dog is around children.

CHAPTER EIGHTEEN
THE IMPORTANCE OF PLAY

"Dogs have boundless enthusiasm but no sense of shame. I should have a dog as a life coach."

- *Moby*

I once played hide and seek with a baby white rhinoceros. This was many years ago, at a wildlife park in Texas.

The baby rhino had been born a few days earlier and, at the time, was one of the only white baby rhinos in the U.S.

When the baby saw me coming, she ran behind her mother. They were in the large pasture together. Her mother was eating alfalfa, so I picked some up and placed it by the fence.

The baby rhino came out from her hiding spot to see what I had put down. I backed off a little to let her explore.

After she had nosed the alfalfa, she looked at me. I bent over a little and swayed back and forth. She started to rock with me. I moved a little to one side; she did the same.

Then, I made what I can only call a "gorilla move." I hunched over and moved in the other direction. She followed. Then we picked up speed.

We ran back and forth like this for ten minutes, bouncing occasionally. At times, she darted behind her mother before looking at me and running off again. We had a glorious time!

I mention this to remind you that animals—and especially dogs—love to play. So do children, as do some adults.

Merging this love of play with the act of training your dog can produce incredible results. This might seem obvious to you, but it is rarely put into practice.

Many dog owners see training and playing as separate activities. But ask yourself this: What does your dog love to do? And how can you leverage that with your training intentions?

Our dog loves Frisbee. She also loves the Chuckit balls and Kong toys and, well, anything she can chase. She especially loves coconuts.

With these props in hand, we taught her the basics of 1 Minute Dog Training— all while having fun.

When I throw a ball, I use a subtle hand signal or my soft voice to practice stay after she retrieves the ball and before she brings it back to me. I count to five or ten, then say (in a complete sentence), "Okay, come on, you good girl."

She gleefully bounds back and waits for the next throw.

Other times, I do this session in reverse. I ask her to please sit or lie down next to me and wait while I throw the Frisbee. Then, when it's high in the air, I say, "Go get it."

She loves the challenge of catching it, which must feel extra rewarding after waiting!

I want to mention that dogs can get injured from too much play. Just like any athlete, you need to be careful if your dog is going to jump for a Frisbee or a ball.

For many breeds, repeatedly jumping high off the ground is not advised. Of course, this is even more important as your dog gets older.

Explore how you can blend play with training. Take note of the games that seem to make you and your dog the happiest, and focus on these activities in your training routine.

CHAPTER NINETEEN
WOOF!

Our dogs can't speak to us in words we understand. Instead, they use a variety of noises to communicate verbally.

Most dogs bark from time to time. Some bark all the time.

Understanding the motive behind your pup's *woofs* is helpful. This way, you can teach him when it is and isn't appropriate to bark.

I Have to Go Outside Bark

This one is self-evident. Hopefully, your dog is house trained and knows how to let you know that he needs to go outside and relieve himself.

If you are still struggling with this issue, I have a House Training Video on my website or you can get my House Training Guide. Scan the QR code or visit **www1.minutedog.com** for more information.

to Watch the House Training Video & Get the Guide

Play Barking

This type of barking is pretty self-explanatory. If your dog barks when she gets excited playing, she's a play barker.

You can inhibit play barking by disengaging from the game when your dog breaks the rules of play (i.e. barking tirelessly).

When your dog barks during playtime, simply remove yourself from the fun. Your pup will quickly learn that barking means playtime is over. She definitely won't want that!

Yelp!

This is your puppy's cry for help. Dogs typically yelp out when they are in pain. This can be physical pain like a broken nail (which dogs are very sensitive to) or emotional distress.

You might hear your dog yelp right after you close the door when you leave to run an errand. That's to be expected.

If, however, you hear your dog yelp at an unexpected time, investigate a bit. It's better to make sure he is okay rather than assume he's being dramatic.

Problem-Solving Problem Barking

When your dog is barking, it may feel natural to engage in a bit of a shouting match. Resist this urge!

Your dog will mirror your energy, so stay calm and take a few deep breaths.

As much as you might want to yell at your dog, this will only spur him on. Your dog will think you're just barking back, which will get him even more riled up.

Instead, rely on what gives your dog confidence. You can try to regain control of the situation by doing a quick sit, stay, come training session with your dog. Dogs usually lose interest in barking if there is an opportunity to focus on something more exciting.

After finding a constructive distraction, I will typically say to my dog in a complete sentence, "Excuse me, that's enough. Would you please stop barking?"

Above all, make sure you don't accidentally reward your dog for barking. Use a focused distraction rather than something that matches your dog's excited energy.

If you start jumping and clapping in an attempt to distract your dog, you might actually reinforce the barking. Your dog will probably think, "Sweet! The more I bark, the more they want to play with me!"

Use a relaxed, focused interruption to distract your dog without rewarding the noisy behavior. Keep calm and do a 1 minute training session with a few TTouches.

Then, reward your dog for all of his good behavior while training.

Communicating Through Body Language

While our dogs can tell us a lot with their voice and their eyes, they also use body language to communicate.

It is important to learn your dog's personal body language cues. This knowledge can allow you to calm your scared or overexcited pup. It could also help you assess potentially dangerous situations.

You can become an expert in reading your dog's body language, but every dog is different.

A raised tail, for example, might look very different for one breed than it would for another. Take this body language guide with a grain of salt, and remember that each dog is a unique individual.

You will learn your dog's particular postures in time. Until then, I've rounded up some of the most common body language cues your dog might use.

Relaxed Dog

When your dog is relaxed, he will appear very soft. His eyes and ears will be in a neutral position. He likely won't have a wrinkled forehead and might even have a slight smile.

His tail will also be level with his spine, although this positioning varies from breed to breed. His body may be wiggly and loose.

If he rolls on his back and offers you his belly, he's looking for love!

In some cases, a fearful dog may show you his belly as a sign of submission. If your pup is showing all of the previously mentioned behaviors, he probably just wants a belly rub.

Scared Dog

A fearful dog will typically cower away with her tail tucked between her legs. Her ears might be pinned back, and she may even be trembling.

Other signs of anxiety in dogs can be more subtle. Some of these signals are excessive yawning, licking her lips (when there is no food nearby), or the "whale eye" (when you can see the whites of your dog's eye).

These indicators can be harder to spot because they seem like normal behaviors. Still, it's best to use soothing techniques just to be sure. The TTouch is a great way to calm a scared puppy.

You can read about other ways to calm a fearful dog on our blog. Visit **1minutedog.com** to learn more.

Playful Dog

The adorable "play bow" is an unmistakable sign of a happy puppy. Your dog's tail will be wagging either level with the spine or higher if she is extra giddy. Her movements might be extra bouncy too.

Note: Dogs often snarl or growl while they are playing. This is a situation where you need to be mindful.

It may be completely normal behavior and does not mean your dog is being aggressive. However, there is a big difference between playful growling and actual aggressive behavior.

If your dog is simultaneously growling and displaying playful behaviors, you need to decide whether or not this is actual aggression. If you are uncertain, please consult with your vet or a dog training professional.

Defensive Dog

It can be difficult to distinguish between an alert dog and an aggressive one. In either case, your dog's hackles (the hair along his back) will likely be raised.

When a dog raises his hackles, he is making himself appear bigger. This is a method of defense. Your dog's fight or flight response may be kicking in here.

Your dog might also appear stiff and could be staring intensely into your eyes. His tail might be sticking straight up and even wagging slightly.

You can sometimes tell if a dog is threatening before he attacks. There are clear warning signs: curled lips, bared teeth, and a growl or snarl. If you experience this kind of behavior, here are a few tips:

- Do not turn and run away, but slowly back off. Speak in a calm, gentle voice. Hold your hand up in a 'stop' position. Avoid making direct eye contact. Remain neutral.
- Again, this is a case where you must be aware of your circumstances. If you are uncertain whether or not your dog is aggressive, please consult with your vet or a dog training professional.

Action Items

- Try to identify why your dog might be barking. Knowing what is causing your dog's barking can help you find the best solution.

- "Listen" to your dog's body language. It's amazing how much our dogs can tell us with their bodies.

- Use these physical cues to help you understand your dog's behavior.

CHAPTER TWENTY
CHOOSING THE RIGHT DOG FOOD

What's a dog's favorite breakfast?

Pupcakes.

I have had many dogs and have worked with lots of people and their dogs. Many of these dogs have had skin conditions and other issues that require various diet changes.

One dog I had developed a pancreatic disorder that made it difficult to digest any type of commercial dog food. For the next 12 years, I diligently made raw food mixed with a bit of rice for her every day.

I would go to the meatpacking plant and buy 100 pounds of raw meat at a time. I would bring it home, mix it together in a wheelbarrow, package it, and freeze it for the next month.

Some months, it was difficult because the main meatpacking plant was over 100 miles away. After she passed, I promised myself I would never go through that again.

When we got our new dog Roxy, a Belgian Malinois, I was convinced I would feed her high-grade, single protein source kibble. As it turned out, Roxy didn't do so well on commercial dog food either.

Check with your veterinarian before changing your dog's diet, especially if your dog has a medical condition.

As we discussed earlier, dogs are genetically similar but behaviorally different than wolves.

Because of dogs' DNA, I feel it is best to follow their ancestral diet. In the wild, that would primarily be raw meat.

In the hectic pace of today's lifestyle, what we feed our dogs comes down to how much time, energy, and money we have. Thus, a dog's diet is subject to the forces of our daily life.

Dog diets can be as diverse as human diets. Consider the optimal human diet consisting of plenty of fresh vegetables, salad, organic whole grains and beans, organic or grass-fed protein, fish, lots of water, and minimal sugar.

On the flip side are fast and fried food, super-size drinks, and processed bread. In the same way, there is a variety of excellent and awful food for dogs.

Suppose you can accept that there is an appropriate diet for humans, which we have fine-tuned through scientific research and evolution.

In that case, you should also be open to the possibility that a dog's diet deserves careful consideration.

Some say dogs can eat anything.

Many dog foods contain chicken or beef by-products. Some claim that animal by-products are nutritionally the same as any other meat; others say, "yuck!"

Animal by-products are left over after all the food humans eat has been harvested from the food source. By-products are considered unfit for human consumption.

Even after being left in a hot trailer for hours, they can still be considered suitable for pet food. These meat by-products are regularly used in dry dog food.[21]

Although considered unusable for human consumption, these by-products are used in dog food because they're cheaper.

I personally will not buy dog food that lists unnamed animal by-products on its label.

If you select a dog food containing by-products, choose a brand with a named by-product meal.

Named by-products specify the source of the protein. This means the ingredient would be listed as "Chicken by-product meal" or "Beef by-product meal," for example.

Avoid purchasing dog food that contains generic by-products. These would be listed as "Meat meal," "Animal by-product meal," or some other non-specific variation.

These by-products have been known to contain a variety of repulsive protein sources.[22]

CHOOSING THE RIGHT DOG FOOD

Simply put, I don't feed my dog kibble with generic animal by-products. I see this as second-rate food.

That being said, I understand it's not realistic for everyone to buy their dog's food from the local butcher and make it at home.

What I do, and you may want to consider, is a holistic diet for your dog that works for your family.

Our family uses raw, grass-fed hamburger, lightly steamed broccoli (which we buy in bulk from Costco), butternut squash, and occasionally raw liver. She also gets a variety of multi-vitamins to ensure she gets a full spectrum of nutrients. If you want more information on this, please visit **1mintuedog.com**.

We have found this works best for Roxy and us! It might require some experimentation to figure out what works best for your family.

Action Items

- Check with your veterinarian prior to changing your dog's diet. Include them in the decision and consider their advice.

- Your vet's knowledge of your dog's health, breed, age, and lifestyle are important factors to recognize.

- Remember that the most expensive food isn't necessarily the better food for your dog.

- When choosing dog food, check the ingredient list. Be sure that any animal byproducts have a named meat source. Avoid generic or unnamed animal byproducts.

- There is a wide range of dog food on the market. There are many terrible things you can feed your dog but very healthy options too.

- Kibble in generally the most affordable and convenient dog food.

- Kibble is also known to contain some very scary ingredients that drive down the price.

- If you purchase dog food that contains animal by-products, please do research beforehand.

CHAPTER TWENTY-ONE
CHOOSING THE RIGHT DOG

"Everyone thinks they have the best dog, and none of them are wrong."

- Unknown

What is it about dogs that makes us love them? Many people would say it's because they give us unconditional love.

Not only do they do this, but they allow us to express our love back to them. This mutual relationship opens our hearts to giving and receiving immense love.

For many people, their relationship with their dog is one of the most important in their lives.

2,000 American pet guardians were surveyed about their relationships with their pets in a 2022 study commissioned by Sealy.

CHOOSING THE RIGHT DOG

The study found that 66% of pet guardians share their beds with their furry friends. And 58% of participants in relationships would rather snooze alongside their pet than their partner![23]

I personally do not invite my dog into my bed, and it's your choice whether to do it or not. But this study confirms something I strongly believe: Dogs are family members! And for many people, they are their whole family.

This is why I created the 1 Minute Dog Training system. I want your family to thrive. I want you to have a straightforward, simple technique that leads to a satisfying result.

Success is the product of small daily habits. We want to have a lifelong relationship with our dogs. This system is a win-win. Your dog will learn, and you will strengthen your relationship.

Even if you and your dog get just 1% better every day, you will see incredible results in just a few weeks or months.

If you already have a dog, there is always room for your relationship and affection to grow.

If you are considering getting a rescue dog or a puppy from a reputable breeder, it is important to be aware of the unique needs of your family and the type of dog you choose.

Knowing what will work for your family allows you to be in a relationship with your dog rather than being the dominant Alpha.

Questions to ask yourself:

- Would this be a good dog for children?
- Is this dog coming with challenges from an abusive past?
- Are you looking for a lap dog? Or someone to go running with you?
- Do you have the time for a high-energy dog (like a retriever or shepherd)?
- Would this dog be suitable for my living situation (apartment, house, van, etc.)?
- Do you have other animals in your household?
- What is the average life expectancy of the breed you are considering?
- Are you allergic to dog dander?
- Do you want a dog for protection?
- What is your experience with dogs or a certain breed?

Take some time to think about the questions above. It can narrow your choices and make this big decision easier.

Please Allow Me to Share One Final Story

I have heard this touching tale repeated many times. There was a ten-year-old Irish Wolfhound named Belker whose family members were Ron, Lisa, and their six-year-old son Shane. They were all in love with Belker!

Sadly, Belker was dying of cancer. They were hoping for a miracle. The family was told there wasn't anything they could do for him.

The veterinarian offered to perform a euthanasia procedure in their home. After agonizing debates and discussions, Ron and Lisa felt it would teach Shane more about life if he were to observe it.

The next day, Belker's family surrounded him. Shane seemed so calm, petting the old dog for the last time. His parents wondered if he understood what was happening. Within a few minutes, Belker slipped peacefully away.

Remarkably, Shane seemed to accept Belker's transition without difficulty or confusion. The family and the vet sat together after Belker's passing, mournful that dogs' lives are so much shorter than the average human's.

Shane, who had been listening quietly, said, "I know why."

Startled, the family all turned to him.

Shane said, "People are born so they can learn how to live a good life—like loving everybody all the time and being nice, right? Well, dogs already know how to do that, so they don't have to stay for as long as we do."

He was right, wasn't he? As you train your dog, remember that the lessons they can teach us are endless.

If dogs were our teachers, the feeling of fresh air and wind on our faces would be pure ecstasy. We'd run, romp, and play daily.

We would thrive on attention and let people touch us; we'd nap without guilt. We'd avoid biting when a simple growl would do.

On warm days, we'd stop to lie and roll around on our backs on the grass; on hot days, we'd chill out under a shady tree.

We'd dance around and wiggle our entire bodies with joy. In search of buried treasure, we would dig and dig until we found it. And if a loved one were having a bad day, we'd be silent, sit close by, and nuzzle them gently.

We'd learn, in the end, the secret to happiness.

Wishing you all the best,

Tom Mitchell

FINAL THOUGHTS

1 Minute Dog Training is not intended to provide individual veterinary advice or diagnosis. You should consult your veterinarian with specific questions or for a specific diagnosis of your dog's health and behavior.

We regret that we cannot respond to individual inquiries about your dog, unless we have established a working relationship. You can contact me through the 1 Minute Dog website.

You can also stay up to date with all the 1 Minute Dog happenings on our social media pages!

 facebook.com/1minutedog/

 instagram.com/1minutedog/

 youtube.com/user/1MinuteDog/

 twitter.com/1minute_dog

I hope you have found this information to be very valuable. I am excited for the progress you will make with your dog moving forward!

In case you ever need a quick refresh about what you have learned, here is a recap for your convenience.

The Three Fundamental Skills of 1 Minute Dog Training

- Sit
- Stay
- Come

What 1 Minute Dog Training Is

- Consistency! It is dedication to strengthening your relationship with your dog.
- A gentle approach to communication through touch, visual cues, and language that demonstrates respect.
- Patience and compassion. It is recognizing that your dog loves you and wants to make you happy.
- A combination of intentional training and enthusiastic play.

FINAL THOUGHTS

- Loads of praise for your dog's outstanding accomplishments!

The 1 Minute Dog Training method is not dominance training. It is not a collection of sharp commands and intimidation.

I encourage you to train with understanding, kindness, and wisdom. I find it's much easier to do this in 1 minute sessions, allowing that understanding to develop over time.

If you assert power over your dog by choking her, being aggressive, or "alpha-ing," as opposed to welcoming your dog as part of the family, you may miss one of the more important relationships in your life.

Can I Ask For a Small Favor?

You now have access to this simple, revolutionary technique in dog training.

I would be incredibly grateful if you took the time to leave a review for this book on Amazon and other social media platforms and book-buying sites. Thank you!

to Get Your Free Videos

I love feedback! Please share what you liked or hoped to learn more about. I truly value your contribution.

To get the absolute most out of this book, I encourage you to utilize your free gift! Please visit **1minutedog.com** to access your FREE exclusive dog training video course.

You can see me and some of my clients in action—this free resource is a great visual representation of my methods.

For all things dog training, check out the 1 Minute Dog website, **1minutedog.com**. Please sign up for special discounts and other books I am working on. I have a lot more to share!

Unfortunately, I cannot answer individual dog training questions unless you are a client. If you'd like to check in with me, however, you may send an email to **info@1minutedog.com**.

You can explore a wide variety of instructional training videos, helpful tips on the blog, more information on my background, and of course, lots of cute dog photos!

Other Books by the 1 Minute Dog Trainer

Involve your whole family in the dog training process! Check out my new dog training book for children! I also have a book on how to Train Your Puppy, a House Training Guide, and lots of blogs. One of my favorite blogs is teaching you how to throw your dog a birthday party! Visit **1minutedog.com** to read more!

to Get the Kids Book

RESOURCES

There are a variety of great tools that can help you train your dog. I have found the most valuable tool to be the Tellington TTouch®.

What is the Tellington TTouch®?

The Tellington TTouch Method enhances the emotional, mental and physical wellbeing of various animals.

It was initially designed for working with horses. I had the privilege to work with Linda Tellington-Jones in the 1980s in Europe with members of Olympic Equestrian teams. We also taught many other clinics together.

The results were so impressive that the Tellington TTouch Method was adapted to work with dogs, cats, rabbits, small beings like guinea pigs, birds, zoo animals, as well as humans.

The mindful, circular movements of the TTouch are very therapeutic for your dog in many ways. How?

Think about it in human terms. Humans use mindful methods—such as taking deep breaths—when we need to collect our thoughts.

When we concentrate on breathing, our mind is focused and cannot wander. This melts away stress and other distractions that prevent us from thinking clearly.

TTouches have a similar effect.

Because we can't ask our dogs to take deep breaths or practice other mindful techniques, the TTouches accomplish this for them. When calm, your dog will learn faster and connect with you on a deeper level.

A dog who feels comfortable and balanced in her body is more confident. This feeling of safety gives your dog a better sense of self-control. The results of such a simple shift are incredible!

Confident, emotionally balanced dogs have better decision-making skills. They are less reactive and, therefore, less likely to show aggressive behavior.

I encourage you to learn more about the Tellington TTouch method. I see incredible results whenever I practice TTouches on my dog and any animal I work with!

When is the Right Time to Practice TTouches?

Any time you have is the right time! I encourage you to do TTouches on your dog before you start a training session, when praising your dog for learning a skill, in situations where your dog seems overwhelmed or anxious, and whenever you have a minute or two of quality time together. Refer to the TTouch website, **ttouch.com**.

What is Clicker Training and How Does it Work?

Many professional dog trainers use the clicker technique. I personally do not use a clicker because I feel that if you do not have one with you, your dog may not listen. This could be especially true in an dangerous moment, such as your dog running out into the road.

I feel it is much better to have your dog listen to your voice than a clicker.

This well-known method is based on "Pavlovian conditioning" or "classical conditioning." Ivan Pavlov, this method's namesake, was a Russian physiologist. In one of his studies, he discovered that dogs learn to associate certain sounds with delicious rewards.

The dogs Pavlov studied not only salivated when they smelled food. They actually began to salivate when they heard the sounds they learned to associate with food.

They knew the research assistant's footsteps meant a meal was on the way, and their mouths started watering. They anticipated the food before it was even brought to them. https://www.simplypsychology.org/pavlov.html

This little history lesson applies to training because Pavlov's observation developed into the clicker method.

If you don't know what a clicker is, it's pretty simple. It is a small hand-held object that makes a single "click!" noise. Many trainers teach young puppies to link the "click!" sound with a reward.

This is accomplished by clicking the clicker very often at first. It is very important to immediately give your dog a treat each time you "click!" Your dog won't need to perform any tricks yet. This is called "charging" the clicker.

You are showing your pup that "click!" means "Yes! Good!"

It is widely believed that Pavlovian conditioning helps dogs learn faster. The clicker marks the exact behavior you want to reward. It basically tells your dog, "Woohoo, that action was great! Now hold on a second while I fish for your treat."

The sound bridges the gap between the action and the reward. This way, your puppy knows precisely what she did right.[24]

That being said, as I mentioned earlier, I do not use a clicker for training dogs. You can still use this effective form of training without buying an actual clicker.

You might use the same word every time you want to mark good behavior. "Yes!" or "Good!" are popular choices. You can also make a "click!" sound or special word with your mouth—you get the idea.

Be consistent with whatever sound you choose. Remember to "charge" this sound the same way you would a clicker. You want your pup to know your sound means she did something right!

What About Tools to Help Your Dog Communicate with You?

By now, we've covered a few different ways you can communicate with your dog through physical touch and sound. But can we encourage our dogs to communicate with us in new ways? Yes!

Many people want their dog to bark as little as possible. While you may appreciate your dog's alert barking it if actually scares away an intruder, the excessive noise is generally bothersome.

There are a variety of tools that allow your dog to communicate with you while keeping the barking to a minimum. Bells by the door, for example, can be your dog's way of telling you: "Let me out, I need to go potty!"

Some dogs are even learning how to "talk" by pressing buttons, which are programmed with words.[25] Dogs can be incredible communicators. We just need to learn how to listen!Different tools may work well for you and your dog.

They will work even better if you establish the 3 basics first:

- Sit
- Stay
- Come

Working with the methods above is most effective in 1 minute sessions. One drawback to training with external methods (such as clickers and treats) is your dog may not listen if you don't have them with you.

You will always have touch, your voice, your bond with your dog, and the 3 basics of sit, stay, and come. Having these tools handy makes them the most valuable ways to connect with your dog in my opinion.

ENDNOTES

1. https://www.apa.org/news/press/releases/2009/08/dogs-think#:~:text=TORONTO%E2%80%94Although%20you%20wouldn't,the%20University%20of%20British%20Columbia.
2. https://www.akc.org/expert-advice/lifestyle/how-do-dog-microchips-work/
3. https://pubmed.ncbi.nlm.nih.gov/27912242/
4. https://cpb-us-w2.wpmucdn.com/about.illinoisstate.edu/dist/6/45/files/2019/10/Severe-brain-damage-after-punitive-training-technique-with-a-choke-chain-collar-in-a-German-shepherd-dog.pdf
5. https://saintfranciswolfsanctuary.org/wolves-as-pets/
6. https://www.amnh.org/exhibitions/permanent/human-origins/understanding-our-past/dna-comparing-humans-and-chimps#:~:text=These%20three%20species%20look%20alike,98.8%20percent%20of%20their%20DNA.
7. https://www.npr.org/transcripts/751492970?storyId=751492970&ft=nprml&f=57
8. https://www.nytimes.com/2019/11/22/science/dogs-love-evolution.html?campaign_id=18&emc=edit_hh_20220214&instance_id=53155&nl=well&regi_id=36483151&segment_id=82702&te=1&user_id=4b88c203cb87b78fdea446127be9ace4
9. https://doi.org/10.1126/sciadv.1700398
10. https://www.sciencedaily.com/releases/2009/02/090217141540.htm
11. https://doi.org/10.1207/S15327604JAWS0304_6
12. https://corporate.petco.com/2020-10-06-Stop-the-Shock-Petco-Ends-the-Sale-of-Electronic-Shock-Collars-Firmly-Establishes-itself-as-the-Health-and-Wellness-Company-for-Pets
13. www.sciencedaily.com/releases/2019/04/190408114304.html
14. https://doi.org/10.7554/elife.55080

ENDNOTES

15 https://www.ncbi.nlm.nih.gov/pmc/articles/PMC7192336/
16 https://www.akc.org/expert-advice/lifestyle/do-dogs-dream/
17 https://www.nature.com/articles/s41598-020-76806-8
18 https://time.com/4775436/how-smart-is-a-dog-really/
19 http://www.sheldrake.org/files/pdfs/papers/Testing-a-Return-Anticipating-Dog-Kane.pdf
20 https://www.avma.org/resources-tools/pet-owners/dog-bite-prevention
21 "The Truth about Animal by-Products in Dog Food." Dog Food Advisor, August 31, 2021.
22 https://www.dogfoodadvisor.com/choosing-dog-food/animal-by-products/
23 https://talker.news/2022/05/18/research-reveals-people-who-share-a-bed-with-their-pet-sleep-better/
24 https://www.akc.org/expert-advice/training/clicker-training-your-dog-mark-and-reward/#:~:text=A%20clicker%20(or%20marker)%20is,your%20dog%20during%20training%20sessions
25 https://www.akc.org/expert-advice/training/how-to-teach-your-dog-to-talk/#:~:text=Using%20buttons%20for%20communication%2C%20you,this%20is%20consistency%20and%20patience.

ACKNOWLEDGEMENTS

I'd like to acknowledge my incredible team for your support through the creation of this book.

For years, I have dreamed about the chance to improve people's relationships with their dogs.

To Kes Lehrman, Olivia Hinchley, and Emma Scott this dream became a reality with your help.

Thank you for your encouragement, insight, and aloha spirit. You are deeply appreciated.

Made in the USA
Las Vegas, NV
11 November 2023

80643523R00095